THE TO

The Lou Groza Story

Lou Groza
with
Mark Hodermarsky

KENDALL/HUNT PUBLISHING COMPANY
4050 Westmark Drive   Dubuque, Iowa 52002

Back cover photo: Cleveland State University Archives

Just For Kicks
Lou Groza
"The Toe"

DEDICATION

To my loving family and to the great sports fans of Cleveland.

Jackie and Lou.

CONTENTS

INTRODUCTION

Joe Montana collected four Super Bowl rings as the quarterback for the San Francisco 49ers; Terry Bradshaw of the Pittsburgh Steelers led his team to the same number of Super Bowl victories. Few professional football players (excluding some of Montana and Bradshaw's teammates) can match this prodigious feat. Yet an offensive tackle/placekicker from an earlier era surpasses this total—by four.

In twenty-one years as a Cleveland Brown, Lou "The Toe" Groza won an astonishing eight championships, four in the All-America Football Conference and four in the National Football League.

Some more facts:

- His Browns teams participated in 13 championship and 3 playoff games;
- He is the only Brown to have played on all eight championship teams;
- He appeared in 9 Pro Bowls;
- 6 times he was chosen All-NFL offensive tackle;
- *The Sporting News* voted him the NFL's Most Valuable Player in 1954;
- He amassed 1608 points (1 TD, 264 FGS, 810 PATs) and is the third leading scorer in professional football history;
- His last-second field goal gave the Browns the NFL title in 1950;
- At his retirement he held 10 NFL records and 24 Browns records;
- He was inducted into the Pro Football Hall of Fame in 1974.

Behind these startling accomplishments, however, is the man himself. Lou Groza's life story reveals a professional athlete of singular dedication, humility, and honor. He symbolizes all that is good about athletic competition—preparation, hard work, selflessness, and duty. Lou reminds us of those earlier legends of sports, Lou Gehrig, Bobby Jones, and Jesse Owens, who performed with consistent brilliance and who never permitted their achievements to fill them with vanity and arrogance. In some ways, Lou Groza's demeanor on and off the football field invokes images of the strong, silent sheriff of the American West, the soft-spoken hero who bravely confronts his foe and then defeats him with a quiet confidence.

Groza played during the golden age of professional football, the late 1940's through the mid-1960's. Most of football's greatest legends played with or against Lou Groza, including Jim Brown, Marion Motley, Otto Graham, Paul Warfield, Johnny Unitas, Gino Marchetti, Ray Nitschke, Joe Schmidt, Y.A. Title, Bob Waterfield, Leo Nomellini, Jim Parker, Chuck Bednarik, Sammy Baugh, George Blanda, Doug Atkins, Roosevelt Brown, Frank Gifford, Sam Huff, Andy Robustelli, and Willie Davis.

During this period, attendance soared as professional football began to compete against college football's prolonged dominance in fan loyalty and fan dollars. The emergence of television accelerated football's appeal by making the game easily accessible to millions of viewers. Television insured the financial feasibility and prosperity of many franchises. Because large profits could be made from owning a team, improved methods of operating football clubs materialized. And the most successful football organization, in winning and drawing fans, was the Cleveland Browns.

Between 1946 and 1967, the Lou Groza Years, the Cleveland Browns dominated their sport like the Yankees controlled baseball, winning more games and more championships than any other professional football team. At this time Cleveland boasted the most Hall-of-Fame players, like Otto Graham and Jim Brown.

The individual most responsible for Cleveland's supremacy was their architect, Paul Brown, who coached the Browns from 1946-1962. Indeed, Paul Brown, more than any single person, made the game of professional football a hugely popular American pastime. Just considering the number head coaches who once played for or coached under Paul Brown demonstrates Brown's impact on the game of football: Don Shula, Bill Walsh, Blanton Collier, Weeb Ewbank, Chuck Noll, Lou Saban, Ara Parseghian, Bud Grant, and Mike McCormack.

When Lou Groza had the chance to play for Green Bay head coach Vince Lombardi in a Pro-Bowl game, Lombardi asked Lou about how Paul might handle certain game situations and about other features of Paul's coaching style. In a sense, all successful coaches "studied" under Paul Brown. The coaching fraternity respected Paul Brown and unabashedly copied many of the components of Paul's system.

Paul Brown's players also respected him. Paul's desire to win, his emphasis on study and preparation, and his keen football mind, inspired his players and one in particular—Lou Groza. Of all the players that Paul Brown coached, Lou Groza was his favorite. A man not noted (at least in public) for becoming attached to his players, Paul often referred to Lou Groza as "my Louie."

Their friendship started at Ohio State (when Paul Brown coached the Buckeyes) where Lou attended school long enough to play in three freshman games before becoming a soldier in World War Two. During the War in the Pacific, Paul kept in touch with Lou by sending him letters, footballs, and, on one occasion, a professional football contract. Paul Brown wanted Lou to play for him in a new league, the All-America Football Conference. And when the war ended that's what Lou did.

Except for a season when Lou couldn't play because of an injury to his back (1960), for the next 21 seasons Lou Groza would revolutionize placekicking and become the most recognizable kicker in the game's history. He would also be remembered as the best clutch kicker of all time. Lou Groza would shatter all of football's kicking and scoring records and establish himself as one of the game's most admired legends.

In the following narrative Lou Groza speaks at length about Paul Brown. Lou also vividly describes: his childhood memories while growing up in a small town (Martins Ferry) along the Ohio River, his war experiences, his many years as a key member of the Cleveland Browns, and his very active post-football years. Lou's anecdotes richly texture his story.

"The Toe" has kicked another game-winner.

Mark Hodermarsky

PART I

STANCE AND APPROACH
From Martins Ferry to Okinawa

In the Shreve High football stadium,
I think of Polacks nursing long beers in Tiltonsville,
And gray faces of Negroes in the blast furnace at Benwood,
And the ruptured night watchman of Wheeling Steel,
Dreaming of heroes.

All the proud fathers are ashamed to go home.
Their women cluck like starved pullets,
Dying for love.

Therefore,
Their sons grow suicidally beautiful
At the beginning of October,
And gallop terribly against each other's bodies.

"Autumn Begins in Martins Ferry, Ohio" by James Wright

"When there is soot on the window sill, there is prosperity," my father used to say. Living across the street from one of our town's three large factories, Laughlin Works, I assumed that Martins Ferry, Ohio was a wealthy place, judging from the expanse of dirt and grime which covered our house. Blaw Knox and Wheeling Steel (Wheeling-Pittsburgh, today) were the other two mills which hurled black clouds and blast-furnace clangs, twenty-four hours a day, into the Ohio Valley skies. But like those who live near airports or railroad tracks will testify, we became so accustomed to the noise that we hardly noticed it. For me, the "prosperity" that my father spoke of actually was generated from the hard-working and good-hearted people of Martins Ferry rather than by her steel mills.

The Ohio River, on whose shores flourished towns like Martins Ferry, Bridgeport, and Bellaire, provided employment, transportation, and recreation. As kids we didn't swim often in those murky waters, but after a neighborhood game of football, baseball, or basketball, we cooled down by jumping carelessly into the Ohio.

In grade school our teachers taught us that Martins Ferry, laid out by surveyor Absalom Martin in 1795 as Jefferson, was Ohio's oldest settlement, We learned that Absalom's son, Ebenezer, transported cattle across the Ohio River on his ferry to Wheeling, West Virginia. In 1835 the town became known as Martinsville in honor of Absalom's enterprising son.   Later the post office changed the name again—this time to Martins Ferry. Our teachers also told us that a well known 19th Century novelist and literary critic, William Dean Howells, was born in Martins Ferry. (Another celebrated writer, the poet James Wright, who graduated with my wife from Shreve High School—or, as it is more often called, Martins Ferry High School— also grew up here.)

Martins Ferry prospered not only economically (at least until recent decades) but also athletically. Despite their small populations, my town and neighboring communities of the Ohio Valley have produced an inordinate number of acclaimed professional athletes—John Havlicek of the Boston Celtics, Bill Mazeroski of the Pittsburgh Pirates, knuckleball artist Phil Niekro and his brother Joe, and Alex Groza. The list also includes Clark Hinkle of the Green Bay Packers and Chuck Howley of the Dallas Cowboys. Notre Dame football coach Lou Holz and Pittsburgh Pirate manager Jim Leyland are Valley Boys as well.

Into this hilly steel town of about 9,000 people, situated in a coal-mining region about sixty miles southwest of Pittsburgh and across the Ohio River from Wheeling, I was born on January 25, 1924.

* * *

In those days doctors delivered babies in the home.   Dr. Messerly, a kindly general practitioner who lived across the railroad tracks, delivered all the Groza children—four boys. All weighed over twelve pounds, the largest babies ever delivered in the Valley. Dad was a huge man, but his children were all taller than him. In fact, I was the smallest of the four boys. John was born first; he was followed by Frank. I was born next and brother Alex arrived after me.

Age one—sitting on my dad's car.

Our family lived upstairs in a four bedroom-house on Main Street above my father's bar, Groza's Tavern, right across from a mill. We lived in the North end of town, about three blocks from the Ohio River.

My father, John, emigrated to this country from Hungary when he was ten years old. He was joined by an older brother, Peter, who worked in nearby Rayland in the Y & O Coal Mine.

When my dad reached middle age, his ankles constantly swelled, making walking painful. My father was 6'1" and eventually weighed over 300 lbs, but as a younger man he was quite agile. A fine baseball player, John Groza would "knock it out of the park" quite regularly at Mill Field according to the old-timers. But he never had the opportunity to develop his skills enough to consider baseball as a career. In those days kids didn't get much of an opportunity to play organized sports. Young boys didn't participate in local baseball leagues, so they got little formal coaching and even less exposure. Pick-up games predominated.

When my dad worked in the coal mines as a young man, he utilized a company mule to remove the coal and slack out of the mine. Once this mule kicked him and blackened his eye. From that point on he was called Big Spot in honor of that incident.

Soon after this event, Dad's brother Peter, in his mid-twenties, was seriously injured in a cave-in at the mine and suffered permanent brain damage. I saw my uncle only once—in a Columbus hospital—and when I visited he didn't recognize me. After this devastating accident to his brother, my dad gave up mining for a living and became a steelworker at Laughlin Works.

A little later, during Prohibition, my father opened a pool hall across from Laughlin Works, and when liquor was legalized he obtained a license and converted the pool hall into a bar and restaurant called Groza's Tavern. My mother did all the cooking, mostly preparing sandwiches and soups, and served all the meals. Groza's Tavern was opened six days a week, 7:00 AM to 12:00 PM, and was closed Sundays. Catering primarily to steelworkers, men would stop in before and after their shifts at work to eat, drink, and play cards. They would also shoot pool and listen to the jukebox. My two older brothers, John and Frank, as they got older, tended bar. Alex and I swept the floor and threw out the trash.

Big Spot didn't take any nonsense from anybody at the bar; he was both owner and bouncer. And John felt very protective regarding his boys. If anybody said anything negative about any of his kids, he defended his sons. Even though we were mostly well-behaved, we occasionally met with our father's disapproval. We feared doing anything wrong because Dad would "lecture" with his belt when we got into any sort of trouble. And those "discussions" hurt.

My father was not the type of sport's fan who perused the sports pages or rooted heartily for a particular college or professional team, but he was deeply interested in following the athletic exploits of his own boys. Dad took Alex and me to watch my older brothers, John and Frank, play football, basketball, and baseball. I remember how people would call Alex and me "Dot and Dash" when we accompanied Big Spot to those games. And when Alex and I reached high school, Dad would always be there to watch us participate.

In 1946, my first year in professional football and the inaugural season of the Cleveland Browns, the players wore brown warm-up jackets with orange lettering. Our names were stitched onto the backs. (One of the best features of the great Browns football tradition, I think, is that their uniform—including the team's colors and distinctively plain helmets—has remained nearly the same for almost fifty years.) After the season concluded we kept the jackets. I gave my jacket to my father after that first year. When my dad would come up for a game the following season, he would proudly don the "Groza" jacket. At times, my performance might have disappointed the home crowd, but fans sitting near my father at Cleveland Municipal Stadium were intimidated by his massive frame and would never dream of booing me.

Unfortunately, my dad never saw me kick that last second field goal in the 1950 title game to give the Browns the NFL Championship. Dad died on June 13, 1950, exactly a month after Jackie and I were married. He was only 62.

When greeting other people, my father advised me to shake hands firmly, to politely say hello and to always "look the other person right in the eye."   Of all his words of wisdom, these last remarks have probably served me best.

My mother's maiden name was Mary Koteles. Like my father, she came to America from Hungary. Unlike my father, Mother was only an infant when she journeyed across the Atlantic. She spoke Hungarian with the neighbors; however, she did not speak broken English.

Mother dedicated her life to serving her husband and children. She fed us quite well—I remember Mom baking as many as six pies for some of our meals. Mom was domesticated, frugal, and pious. When my father died, she didn't remarry. Remarriage would rarely occur in those days, so she never considered finding another spouse.

When my father died in 1950, we asked Mom if she wanted to sell the business, and she replied, "No. All my friends are here and they often come in to see me." The tavern was not only her livelihood but also her recreation. A friend helped Mom run Groza's Tavern, but my mother's declining health made it increasingly difficult for her to operate the tavern. Our tavern was eventually sold, and my brother and I sold the place and moved Mom uptown. Years later the tavern was torn down.

Mother later developed a diabetic ulcer on her foot, and some doctors considered amputating her foot. Luckily the operation was not needed. I asked her to move up to Berea and live with my family, but she wouldn't. She wished to stay near her friends in Martins Ferry.

Mother died in the winter of 1976, two years after my induction into the Pro Football Hall of Fame.

*   *   *

Our mixed neighborhood reflected the immense traffic of immigrants reaching the American shores at the turn of the century. Work easily could be found in the mines and mills of the Ohio Valley. Greeks, Hungarians, Polish, Italians, and blacks (in addition to other nationalities and races) lived in my neighborhood. Our family attended St. Mary Catholic Church, while many of our other neighbors worshipped elsewhere.

As a kid we didn't have a playground, but we did have Mill Field which was located between Laughlin Works and the Ohio River. No grass grew on the playing surface. And ash from the blast furnaces, rising in heaps at the adjacent cinder dump, dispersed scads of dust. The field would get muddy when the river rose and, subsequently, become dry and cracked as the waters resided. (Despite the rough surface, the fabled Homestead Grays of the Negro Leagues, led by legendary catcher Josh Gibson, once played on this diamond during one of their barnstorming tours. I remember the "collection hat" being passed among the spectators.)

Other than at Mill Field, we used to entertain ourselves in one of the neighbor's yards, usually the neighbor who had the nicest grass. (Louie Bevilacqua and Orlando Pratti, two childhood pals, and I used to chum around quite a bit. The kids that I hung out with ended up being my teammates in high school and friends for life.) We also played near or in the water. Some of the bolder kids would try to swim across the Ohio. I recall at least one boy who had failed to reach the other side and had drowned. Plus we used to throw and kick a football on Avondale Street, which intersected Main Street. To this day I can read my initials (L. G.) which I carved into a concrete curb on Avondale.

We played basketball in an open space in the yard of a black church. We found some unused railroad ties and nailed down a couple of baskets on top of those ties. "Rough and tumble" accurately describes our basketball contests. Always being big for my age, I used to play with the older kids. I think that this helped to develop my abilities because I had to fight and scratch while I played. Those were real knock-down-drag-out games.

And that's the way it was in anything that we did— whether it was baseball, basketball, or football. We played tackle football without pads when we were kids. We had to make our own recreation and our own fun. Organized sports didn't really start until high school.

Like my father, I didn't follow any particular college or professional team. I once went up to see the Pirates play Cincinnati at Forbes Field and saw Ernie Lombardi belt a home run for the Reds. Pittsburgh was only sixty miles from Martins Ferry, so to travel to Cleveland or to Cincinnati was a major trip in those days. In fact, the first professional football game that I saw was the one that I first played in.

Across the river rose the only big city that we knew much about— Wheeling. Any major shopping had to be done here. We sometimes drove north along the river to Steubenville to listen to the big bands perform the very popular "Swing" sound of that era. My family never went to many places when we were growing up, except to the occasional Sunday family picnic at Reasbeck's Farms. Hungarian music filled the air as we children played tag, dodging in and around the dancers.

I enjoyed school. I was a good student—studious, disciplined, self-motivated. I was not a troublemaker because I was always afraid of doing anything wrong and embarrassing my parents or incurring my father's wrath. Yet I was very quiet and still am, although not to the same degree. Unlike my brothers, I was hesitant to enter into conversations. My mother was afraid that I wouldn't do well in school because I was so shy. She was afraid that I wouldn't answer the questions posed by my teachers. I really had to work hard to conquer my shyness.

I'll never forget one teacher, Miss Knapp. On her birthday, she stepped out of her classroom, leaving her students alone. Because of my respect for her, I uncharacteristically (despite my shyness, in other words) began to solicit contributions to buy Miss Knapp a present. She suddenly returned and noticed me out of my seat and concluded that I was a rabble rouser. I melted under her glare. Fortunately for me and everyone else in that room, she later understood why I had been standing instead of sitting. An excellent teacher and role model, Miss Knapp attended all of our games at Martins Ferry and was probably our most loyal fan.

Besides my father, mother, and brothers, those who made the deepest impression on me were my coaches, teachers, and, in particular, Frank Bowen, the athletic director at Martins Ferry High School. Bowen's enthusiasm for sports and for life rubbed off on me.

* * *

My oldest brother John, who graduated from Martins Ferry High School in 1934, played center on the basketball team and tackle for the football team, but unlike the next Groza boys—Frank and Lou— he was not a kicker. When John was in high school my parents bought him a coronet for the marching band. They didn't want John to play football because they were afraid that he might get hurt. Well, John came home once with a black eye and admitted lying to them about being in the band. I have the impression that my dad was secretly delighted about John's confession.

John stood 6'3" tall and weighed about 220 lbs. At West Virginia University as a freshman football player, he tore up his knee. Joe Stydahar, a future Hall-of-Fame tackle with the Chicago Bears, replaced my brother at WVU. In those days, if you weren't playing you didn't stay in school, so John returned home. The injury kept John out of the service.

He would later open a tavern in Lancaster, Ohio, where a heart attack would eventually claim his life.

Andy Koteles, an uncle who once kicked for Martins Ferry High School, taught the art of placekicking to my older brother Frank. Slightly larger than John, Frank went about 6'4" and weighed 225 lbs. Like John, Frank played the tackle position, but, unlike his older brother, Frank kicked for the Martins Ferry Purple Riders.

Frank was really my first kicking instructor. As youngsters Frank and I used to kick the ball back and forth to each other. Compared to my efforts, Frank's kicks would sail long and beautifully as I chased his lengthy boots. Frank patiently showed me (among other kicking fundamentals) how to kick a spot on the ball. He told me that "the kicking toe should come into contact with the lower third of the ball." With his advice I soon began kicking the ball with greater distance and accuracy. I used to practice my placekicking with Frank by kicking a football over some telephone wires (for lack of goalposts) at Mill Field.

Besides teaching me how to kick a football properly, both Frank and John taught me the fundamentals of blocking. I learned about the three-point and the four-point stances. Although I achieved more fame as a kicker, I always grade high in blocking statistics. I was named All-Pro tackle six times in the thirteen years (1947-1959) that I blocked for the Browns. Despite being recognized more often for my kicking accomplishments, I was inducted into the Pro Football Hall of Fame as an "Offensive Tackle and Placekicker."

Like my father, Frank was a very good baseball player. A slugging first baseman, Frank graduated from high school in 1938 and went on to play minor league ball in Johnstown, Pennsylvania, in the Mid-Atlantic League. Frank probably could have gone on to the majors, but he hurt his shoulder one year and came home to recuperate. Frank then joined the Air Force for what he thought would be one year. Before World War II, men often enlisted in a branch of the armed services for one year. (I remember a song of that era, "See You in a Year.")

In December of 1941, however, the Japanese extended the enlisted man's length of duty by attacking Pearl Harbor and forcing the United States to enter into the conflict. Ironically, Frank was just about ready to leave the service when the war broke out. He was, now, in for the duration, serving in the ground crew at New Caledonia, an island in the South Pacific. Frank did play major league ball—in a sense. He played a lot of baseball in the service with some major league baseball players. But when the war finally ended, Frank thought that he was too old old to resume a baseball career, and he lived in Martins Ferry until his untimely death from cancer. My mom was still alive to grieve over Frank's passing.

Younger brother Alex was an All-American basketball player, one of the University of Kentucky's "Fabulous Five." Tallest of the four Groza sons, Alex rose 6'7" and weighed 235 lbs. He was college basketball's player of the year in 1948 and was voted Most Valuable Player of the National Collegiate Championships in two consecutive years (1948 and 1949) when he led Adolph Rupp's teams to back-to-back national titles. In three seasons at Kentucky, Alex's teams were 34-3, 36-3, and 32-2. My brother also helped the U.S.A. win the gold medal in basketball in the 1948 Summer Olympics. He went on to play professional basketball for the Indianapolis Olympians. (And I used to always tease him that he used to sit the bench on our high school team when I was a senior and Alex was a sophomore.)

Many years before his recent death from cancer in San Diego, Alex had been a loving husband, a dedicated father, a fine basketball coach (at Bellarmine College), and a successful businessman.

* * *

Growing up I inherited the nickname "Big Chief." When I was just a little kid, I faithfully listened to a radio program that aired at about

4 or 5 o'clock—*Chief Wolf Paw*. The show opened with a mesmerizing tom-tom of " Boom, Boom, Boom, Boom, Boom . . ." The producers of the radio show offered an incentive for listening. If you sent in Wrigley Gum wrappers, you'd get a jacket with a wolf paw on it. So I saved up some wrappers, sent them in, and received a Wolf Paw jacket, a pullover with buttons and an imprint of a wolf's paw. I often wore this jacket, so my friends and family began calling me Big Chief or just Chief. People back home in Martins Ferry still call me Big Chief or Chief.

As a sophomore in high school I stood 6' 1" and weighed 210 lbs; I was much larger than most of my teammates and opponents. I also benefited from learning how to block and kick from brothers John and Frank. Frank's kicking instructions, particularly, began to pay dividends for me. I was now able to kick a football over a wall fifty yards beyond the goalposts at one end of our high school football stadium. And at the other end of the field I soon could kick a ball beyond those goalposts and over a fence and onto the railroad tracks.

For the Martins Ferry Purple Riders I won ten letters in high school (4 in baseball, 3 in basketball, and 3 in football) and was captain on all three teams—football, basketball, and baseball. But my greatest thrill involved basketball. Our basketball coach, Floyd Baker, had some success at Bridgeport High School before he came to Martins Ferry. It was unheard of for a Valley team to go to the state tournament, and Baker had taken Bridgeport to the state tournament on several occasions. In my junior year in 1941, we won the Ohio High School Basketball Championship. (The only time that Martins Ferry, before or since, has captured a state basketball crown.) I was voted All-Ohio center and MVP in the state tournament, earning my very first trophy and receiving a basketball with "MVP" inscribed on it.

In the afternoon semi-final against Xenia Central, the score was tied, 34-34, with only seconds remaining in the game, when a Xenia Central player was dribbling up the court. I was guarding the center, and I saw out of the corner of my eye that the man with the ball was going to pass the ball to the guy I was guarding. Well, I intercepted the pass, passed the ball to a teammate, and raced down the floor. My teammate returned the ball to me near our basket, and as the buzzer went off and as I released the ball, the defender hit my hand and knocked the ball away. I was fouled.

The game was not quite over. I was preparing to ask my coach, Floyd Baker, if we should take the ball out of bounds or shoot the free throws. In those days you had that option. But then I realized that we couldn't take the ball out of bounds because the game was over—no time remained. I was given two foul shots after time had expired. Alone on the court, I looked over at our very pale head coach. I was the worst foul shooter on the team. I tossed the first free throw and it surprisingly went through the net, and I then flipped in the second one. We would participate in the state championship game that night.

The Ohio State Championship game was played before a full house at the fairgrounds in Columbus. We beat Lakewood, 37-30, in the finals that evening. Interestingly, Cliff Lewis, a future teammate with the Browns, starred on that Lakewood team. Cliff and I would always discuss that game. He thought, of course, that his team was better and should have won. The Lakewood squad certainly had the look of champions, showcasing a big, purple-and-gold water wagon at the game. (Cliff's father had built this fancy unit.) Conversely, to cool ourselves, the Martins Ferry team shared a dirty, old towel.

Coming home as state basketball champs, while our athletic director, Frank Bowen, was driving, my buddy Louie Bevilacqua and I were sitting in the front seat of the car. Bowen couldn't fathom why his car was going so fast; he was a slow driver. And here, Lou, sitting in the middle, was pressing down on the gas pedal with his left foot.

We journeyed triumphantly home from Columbus through a neighboring town in the Valley, St. Clairsville. When we got to the foot of St. Clairsville Hill, on Route 40, the Martins Ferry fire engine appeared. The firefighters of the community met us and put the entire basketball team on the hook-and-ladder and drove us into town. The Martins Ferry Marching Band was present as was a young beauty named Jackie Lou Robbins, my future wife. Her mother wanted Jackie to see the parade and to join in the celebration. (Jackie is five years younger than me, and I really didn't know her at this time.) Jackie's mother knew the Groza family and brought her daughter to greet the champions. The festivities concluded in Martins Ferry as the band, fire engine and accompanying paraders road past Groza's Tavern on Main Street, the only time in my life that a parade had passed in front of my house.

In 1942 in basketball we didn't return to the state championships largely because during district action, while leaping for a rebound, I fell and hit my head on the floor, knocking myself out cold. My high school basketball days ended on that play.

The guys from that 1941 team went on to other successes. Bob Bowen played basketball and tennis at Ohio State and later went into dentistry. Manager Bill Crump also became a dentist. Billy Elias later coached at Navy. Bob Forsythe, one of the trainers, became the chief architect on the Pro Football Hall of Fame in Canton, Ohio. And Bill Young's jersey number (#44) was retired after his senior year.

Our baseball team, on which I played first base like my brothers, just missed making it to the state finals. We were crowned district champs, however.

Martins Ferry religiously supported its athletic teams. Bellaire and Wheeling were out two biggest rivals, and our football stadium was always packed for those meetings. Games were played on Fridays under the lights, and a few Saturday afternoon games sprinkled the schedule. Attending high school football games was the favorite pastime of the residents of Martins Ferry.

Earlier in my junior year, our Purple Riders football team won the school's first and only state title in football. We actually shared the title with Toledo Libbey, who tied us at their field (14-14) in a contest billed as the state championship.

I was an all-state tackle on both sides of the line, and I did all the kicking. We didn't kick many field goals, but we always kicked extra points. One game that season stands out . I hit three field goals as we defeated Bellaire High School, 9-0. Following the win I received my very first game ball.

In my senior year three football games were decided on kicks. Trailing 14-12 to Bellaire, with time running out, on a fourth-and-eight situation, the center snapped the ball over my head as we attempted to kick the winning field goal. I dashed back to retrieve the ball and carried it just far enough forward to get the first down. Eventually I kicked the game-winning field goal as we won, 15-14.

I played both offensive and defensive tackle (as well as kicker) for my high school team—the Martins Ferry Purple Riders. Here I am in my three-point stance.

I had three different high school football coaches. When I was a freshman, we were led by John Cox, a professorial type, who later became a dentist. Coach Cox thought he'd try me out at fullback. In our first scrimmage I took a hand off and a player missed a block about five yards away, leaving me unprotected. A linebacker then crashed solidly into me, breaking my thigh board and giving me a painful charley horse. From that point I started playing left tackle, the position I played throughout my career. I didn't want to play anywhere else—I was satisfied just to play. My physical dimensions suited me for the position.

When I was a sophomore, Cy Letzeller, an assistant coach at Army and a resident of Martins Ferry, paid me a visit. Cy impressed me as a coach and as a person, so I started to think that I would attend West Point after I graduated from high school. World War II soon broke out and I lost contact with Cy, so I dropped my plans of becoming a cadet.

Doc Hartwig, an All-American guard at the University of Pittsburgh in 1934, became the football coach during my sophomore year. Later he went back to Pitt to coach. In my junior and senior year Gomer Jones, an All-American center at Ohio State in 1935, coached us. Gomer went on to become an assistant to Bud Wilkinson at Oklahoma before replacing Bud as the head coach.

Floyd Baker, my basketball coach, took me aside and discussed the importance of being a good student and described the opportunities that awaited me in college. I maintained excellent grades and made the National Honor Society. I could have attended a lot of schools; I received offers from all over the country. Notre Dame, Ohio State, Penn State, Pittsburgh, and Michigan all showed interest.

After my senior football season ended in 1942, Gomer Jones, Albert Dix (who owned the newspaper in town), and I were visited by some coaches from Ohio State. This was my first meeting with Paul Brown, who the following Fall would lead the Buckeyes to their first national championship. Paul Brown, a couple of years before, was recognized as the greatest high school coach in the country for his record of achievement at Massillon, Ohio. I was left alone in a room as Coach Brown and his assistant coaches asked me all sorts of questions.

Afterwards, they told me what they could do for me if I decided to go to Ohio State: "Lou, the best we can do for you is to offer you a full football scholarship and to give you a varsity job paying fifty dollars a month." I thought that this was a fair offer. And I especially liked the fact that Columbus was close to home.

One other point needs to be mentioned. In high school one of my coaches strangely told me not to major in physical education in college because I was Catholic. Although he didn't directly state his aversion to Catholics, he was reflecting the prejudice that some locals held toward those of us who were Catholic. Despite the large number of Catholics in town, white crosses from the Ku Klux Klan (KKK) sometimes burned on a hill near Martins Ferry. This coach's suggestions, no doubt, affected my decision to major in marketing at Ohio State instead of physical education.

Preparing for the future was a trait which I began to develop at this time. This quality has provided comfort and security for me and my family. As a freshman at OSU in the Fall of 1942, I wasn't sure about my future beyond college. I knew a professor who was a football fan, and I asked him, "How do you know what you want to do when you get out of college?"

"Lou, sometimes guys don't even know what they want to do even after they are working. They still don't know what they want to do. Find something that you think you are interested in and go after it."

For my varsity job, I worked at David Davies Meat Company in Columbus. And the first challenge was finding its location. I didn't know my way around Columbus too well, and I always worried about getting off the bus at the wrong spot. For a couple of hours a day after football practice, I helped load sides of beef onto trucks. There I met Bill Willis, a future teammate and Hall-of-Famer. He was the first varsity player at Ohio State that greeted me. Willis was a lean, muscular guy, and he could pick up that half of beef with little problem. I couldn't figure out how he was able to pick up that beef so easily while I, who was much bigger, struggled. And he finally showed me his secret. Bill taught me how to balance the weight in a way which lessened my exertion.

Paul Brown didn't see me much since I was on the freshman team and he was the varsity coach. But despite focusing his attention on his own team, which was hunting for a national title, Paul (when he could) also took careful notice of the Buckeye freshmen. This quality along with a superb memory gave Paul an edge over most football strategists. The only time Paul would see me would be after his own team's practice had ended. After lining up, we'd practice kicking on an adjacent field. I could see Paul, gazing intensely with binoculars, high up in the open end of Ohio Stadium from the training room, watching me kick. I guess he never forgot the accuracy and length of my practice kicks.

My freshman coach at Ohio State, Ernie Godfrey, was very sincere and worked diligently. After the football season was over, during the middle of winter, he took me under his wing. He would practice kicking with me, several times a week, while we met under the big horseshoe, Ohio Stadium. Most significantly, he taught me how practice improves capabilities.

The varsity Buckeyes under Paul Brown won Ohio State's first national championship, but Brown lost most of his talented kids to the service in 1943, as World War II escalated. His 1943 team, in fact, was nicknamed "The Baby Bucks."

Our Buckeye freshman team played three games. I kicked five field goals in our wins over Indiana, Pittsburgh, and Michigan. We played Michigan and Pitt in Columbus, and Indiana in Bloomington. On our freshman team was Tony Adamle who later became a Brown. Ahead of me, on the varsity, were several important members of the first Browns team: Bill Willis, Tommy James, Dante Lavelli, Bob Gaudio, Gene Fekete, and Lin Houston. In a sense, Ohio State became the Cleveland Browns farm team in those early years.

At the end of my freshman year at Ohio State I was drafted into the Army. For the next few years, 1943-1945, surviving the war took precedence over my interest in football. I would spend most of my time in the South Pacific, dodging bullets and treating wounded soldiers, while witnessing the horrors of war.

* * *

I was inducted into the Army at Fort Hayes in Columbus. Heading west (destination unknown) the next day on the same train sat a number of Buckeye football standouts and future Cleveland teammates, including Tommy James and Dante Lavelli. Our train eventually stopped in Chicago, next to a trainload of German prisoners. The two trains were heading in opposite directions. But the major difference between the two vehicles became clear from the behavior of those German soldiers. They were singing and having a great time. In contrast, every American soldier on our train was solemn. We knew we were heading toward the battleground, while the German prisoners were enjoying the fact that the war had finished for them.

While Dante Lavelli ended up at Camp Walters, Texas, and later at the Battle of the Bulge, Tommy James and I wound up in Camp Barkley in Abilene, Texas. Red dust gusted everywhere. Basic training lasted three months. My next objective was to go to Officer Candidate School (OCS) after spending a portion of my duty in the Medical Replacement Training Center. The Army, however, said that I couldn't achieve OCS status until I was permanently assigned, so I was then sent to Brooks General Hospital in San Antonio, Texas, with the idea of becoming a surgical technician. I finally got permanently assigned to a station hospital in Camp Ellis, Illinois, when I again applied for OCS.

At Camp Ellis, a lieutenant asked me, " Why do you want to do this (OCS) when you could go to college?"

"What's the program?" I asked.

He replied, "The Army's specialized training program."

I then asked, "How do you enroll?"

He returned, "You have to pass a test to get in."

The program sounded good. At this time I was a sergeant, having been in the Army for about four months. So I went to the University of Illinois and took a test, and was accepted into the program.

I attended Bradley Tech (today, it's Bradley University) for the next five months, earning college credits, until they disbanded this course. (So much for heeding the advice of military superiors.) All of us in the program subsequently became soldiers in the 96th Infantry Division. Most of my friends at Bradley were in the infantry and became members of various ground forces. These guys did most of the dirty work, and their lives were often in more jeopardy than was mine. I was lucky to have had the surgical technician's training, so I wound up in a medical battalion.

We stored a football in our Post Exchange (PX) Box, our recreation equipment. But we didn't remove any of the equipment until after the battle was over and won.

When we finally had time for recreation, we played touch football, or we played kicking games like kicking the pigskin back and forth to one another. We kicked and threw the ball around, regularly inventing different kicking games.

The only competitive football that I played in the service was in the Army specialized training program at Bradley. We were divided into

My World War II Army photograph.

two groups—Company A and Company B. And everything we did was against the other company. We played basketball, football, and other sports, but we played only one game of tackle football when the people at Bradley somehow were able to get uniforms.

I recall developing a friendship with Roy Fraleigh, who played football at Michigan State. He was my main opponent on the other company's line. Our friendship sadly didn't last too long as Roy was killed in the war. In 1944, Roy was cut in half by machine gun fire while on patrol on Leyte Island during the Pacific Campaign.

In late 1943 I went to Hawaii for jungle training. Being new in the outfit the Army sent us to an area where we were going to teach infantrymen how to apply splints and bandages. It was actually as nice a duty as our outfit ever enjoyed. We worked three days, then were off the fourth. Of course, when the first sergeant saw what a soft duty we had, we made up for it by being assigned the more difficult details, like boxing and loading heavy equipment onto a ship. This detail lasted only a short while because we were now preparing to sail into combat.

Weeks later we're on a ship, among a convoy of boats, heading to Yap Island in the West Pacific, east of the Phillipines. En route, however, the orders were changed to go to the Admiralty Islands, south of the Equator. (Unexpected shifts in destinations were commonplace.) To lift our spirits, the ship would land on shore every once in a while. A lot of guys drank beer and gladly received beer rations on land. We played ball and you'd get all sweaty and go back to the ship and take a not-so-refreshing salt water shower.

In October of 1944, our ship sailed to a more specific location, but we still didn't know precisely where we were going. There weren't many ships in our convoy, so we assumed that this must not be a very big operation. Finally, when we were two days out of the Phillipines our superiors announced that we were going to be part of the invasion forces in the Leyte Gulf in the Phillipines. Our invasion time was called "HR plus Two" (at Leyte), meaning the invasion was to begin two hours after the first troops had landed. You couldn't have picked a rougher time in which to storm a beach.

When we arrived in Leyte, as far as you could see were stretched lines of ships. Then it came time to climb down the rope ladders to hop in the boats which would carry us to shore. Some guys were so paralyzed with fear that they fell from the ladders into the water in panic. While we hastened down the ropes and into the boats, Japanese Kamikaze planes were crashing violently into many of the ships. What an unforgettable spectacle.

Finally, with the fumes from the boat making me so nauseous that I was glad to get off the boat, I jumped into the water. After I waded to the shoreline, prepared to charge onto the beach, I was momentarily and unforgettably transfixed. The very first thing that I saw on the beach was a dead American soldier whose face had been hideously blown apart. Almost as disturbing to me was the realization that someone had gone through his wallet and had taken his money.

I was a surgical technician in a medical battalion. We were the first surgical unit (medical installation) to bring the wounded back. That was probably as tough a part of the war that a boy of my age could get involved in. Lots of wounded and dead scattered the beach. The screams from the wounded particularly frightened me. But we had work to do, and I was able to collect myself and do my job. We tried to set up a station, like a MASH. (A MASH was more plush, in comparison, because we operated in tents.)

We also worked under an oath which promised that if the enemy ever broke through our lines, then we couldn't run away and leave our patients. We had to stay with our patients under any circumstance.

I remember a Kamikaze plane that crashed about a hundred yards away. A lot of GI's ran over there, but most of us exercised caution, suspecting that the plane was booby trapped. The dead Japanese pilot was still clutching his country's flag as he slumped in the crunched cockpit. Few soldiers would dare risk their lives to remove this souvenir from the Kamikaze pilot's grip.

Amid the confusion of battle, some of us became separated from our outfit, and in the approaching darkness we got lost. Then a bulky Filipino appeared out of nowhere. He couldn't speak English, so we didn't know at first if he were Japanese. But since he was walking behind our lines, we assumed that he probably was on our side. He pulled out a machete, climbed a tree, and cut down some coconuts for us to eat that night. We dug in on the beach and found our outfit the next day.

For some reason being a medical soldier I was assigned the duty of loading artillery shells on a ship. One time as I waited for a truck-load to come, reading a Martins Ferry paper that I got in the mail, a soldier drove by in a jeep, stopped, and stared. He was a friend from Martins Ferry. I knew he was from home because he called me "Chief." Actually I was reunited with four or five acquaintances from Martins Ferry (including my old friend Lou Bevilacqua) while I was in Leyte and Okinawa.

In April of 1945, our division was sent to Okinawa. As a surgical technician, I was part of the first medical installation which received the wounded. As in Leyte, I saw it all, including countless young men wounded and killed in battle. We were about two and one-half miles behind the front lines all the time. The war matured me. I started to realize that there were lots of other things to think about rather than the good things in life. Somehow I got accustomed to it. I accepted things that I would have never accepted before.

I remember treating one soldier who got hit by shrapnel in the back at Okinawa, and his outfit brought him back for medical assistance. He was all muddy and he says, "Hi Lou." I looked at him and recognized him as someone I met at Bradley Tech. The doctor took me aside and told me that this guy was extremely lucky. All the bone had been sheared away from his spinal cord. A hair more and he would have been paralyzed.

Not until July 5, 1945, when General MacArthur announced the liberation of the Philippines, did I seriously look at my future. Paul Brown would help to determine those post-war plans.

PART II

CONTACT
A Cleveland Brown

"Lou Groza exemplifies everything I like and admire about a football player."

Paul Brown

Organized by Arch Ward, the sports editor of the Chicago *Tribune* who helped establish baseball's All-Star Game and the College Football All-Star Game, in 1946 a new league—The All-America Football Conference—was launched. Ward's intentions seemed clear. He wished that football would have two leagues like major league baseball (American and National) and that eventually the winners of each league would play against each other in a (one-game) World Series of football. Twenty years later, Arch Ward's vision would come true when the NFL-Green Bay Packers defeated the AFL-Kansas City Chiefs, 35-10, in the first Super Bowl.

Paul Brown had decided to coach professional football instead of continuing as the head man at Great Lakes Naval Training Station, where he guided his teams to a 15-5-2 mark in two seasons. In his final game as a college head coach in 1943, Paul Brown's Great Lake's team shocked the college football world by upsetting a powerful Notre Dame squad, 19-14. (Despite this loss to Great Lakes, the Irish won their 4th national title.) In three seasons at Ohio State Paul's teams went 18-8-1 and won a national championship in 1942, in only his second year of college coaching. Earlier in nine years at Massillon (Ohio) High School, Paul compiled a 81-7-2 record, building Massillon into America's most fabled high school football town.

At the end of my Army stint, as the war was coming to a close, my former high school coach, Gomer Jones, invited me to attend the University of Oklahoma when I returned to Martins Ferry after the war. Gomer thought that I could finish college and play football with Bud Wilkinson, who had just taken over the program and who later would coach the Sooners to three national championships. A more enticing opportunity, however, soon appeared—a chance to play for the coach I respected the most, Paul Brown, and to earn money and go to college, all in one package.

Coach Brown kept in touch by writing letters to me when I was stationed in Leyte and Okinawa. He also sent me footballs and a pair of football shoes. (When I had the opportunity, I practiced my kicking with Paul's footballs in jungle clearings.) In Okinawa I opened up one of these letters to discover a professional football contract . With little deliberation on my part, I signed the contract and mailed it back to him. I did not understand that the contract may not have been legal, given my college status. In those days a player wasn't suppose to sign a contract until his college class had graduated.

Ohio State athletic director Lynn W. St. John wasn't pleased that his former coach was wooing young men who still had years of college eligibility remaining. Paul Brown argued that he could sign these returning soldiers because, in essence, their classes had already graduated during the war, making these men eligible to sign professional contracts. And the contracts included a stipulation that we must finish our college educations during the off-season. With that, I, along with other war veterans like Dante Lavelli, Gene Fekete, Tommy James, and Tony Adamle, became eligible to sign contracts.

When I was discharged in February of 1946, Paul Brown arranged for me to meet with an assistant coach, John Brickels, in Martins Ferry to sign a new, more detailed contract. This would be the first of twenty-one contracts which I signed with the Browns. Every year I signed a one-year contract. I never liked the idea of multi-year contracts because I always wanted to negotiate on the performance of my previous year. Even when the Browns offered me a multi-year contract I wouldn't sign one.

I got paid $7,500 my first year. That was big money at that time. Some of the guys (linemen) playing before the war were getting fifty dollars a game in the NFL. Under contract with the Browns, I went back to Ohio State to complete my freshman year of studies. And I continued to attend Ohio State in the off-season and earned a degree in marketing in 1949. From that point on, I lived in Berea, a southwestern Cleveland suburb.

Paul Brown began signing players that he had coached or had coached against: Otto Graham, Marion Motley, Bill Willis, Mac Speedie, and Lin Houston. From the Cleveland Rams, who had just beaten the Sammy Baugh-led Washington Redskins for the 1945 NFL Championship, 15-14, Paul grabbed Tom Colella , Don Greenwood, and Chet Adams. Paul promised that he wouldn't raid the Cleveland Rams for players unless the Rams moved out of Cleveland. Because of paltry attendance figures (in four home games the Rams only drew 73,000 fans) owner Dan Reeves moved his franchise to Los Angeles, leaving some of his players susceptible to Paul Brown's offers. From other NFL teams Paul persuaded Lou Rymkus of the Washington Redskins and Edgar Jones and Jim Daniell of the Chicago Bears to become Browns. Professional football's greatest dynasty began to take shape.

In July of 1946 I was off to training camp in Bowling Green, Ohio, wearing Army fatigues and carrying a duffel bag.

* * *

Paul Brown professionalized football. I don't suggest that he created professional football; NFL football had been around since 1920. I mean that Paul Brown was the first coach to develop a precisely organized system of operation, not unlike those found in the plans of successful corporations.

For example, Paul was the first head coach to hire a full-time staff; they worked all year round. In the past, coaches and players would serve on a part-time basis and would report to training camp in the early autumn for a couple of weeks to prepare for the exhibition and regular season contests. Training camp began earlier (July) when Paul joined professional football, so players had to work out more diligently during the off-season in order to arrive in proper condition.

To stay in shape during the off-season, in May and June of every year, I would travel from my home to the Berea High football field to kick and run laps. (The Browns moved to Berea about four years after I retired. The irony is that for all those years we'd practice on the East Side at League Park or Case Western Reserve University.)

Some coaches used to employ *Street and Smith's,* a popular college football preview magazine, during the college draft because this publication offered specific scouting reports on many college standouts. Instead of relying on magazines like *Street and Smith's*, however, Paul asked his coaches to scout. Paul also personally contacted college coaches about different football players. He based his decisions about a football player on firsthand observations made by highly competent judges of talent, rather than relying on newsstand studies. In the process Paul Brown created the modern scouting system.

The fact that Paul Brown paid his coaches and players a good salary also contributed to his success. Professional football players, at least under Brown, could now earn enough money to play football for a living. Before Paul arrived many college stars refused to play professional football because they found more lucrative futures in other jobs. And because the Browns offered good money to their players, to compete against Paul's team, other franchises began to increase salaries.

The Browns were one of the first professional football teams to travel across the country on chartered planes. We enjoyed first-class service and accommodations wherever we went, inaugurating the way modern professional sports franchises treat their athletes.

Paul was the first coach to use notebooks and classroom techniques, to organize film study, to grade player's performances, and to give intelligence tests.

Brown was quite an innovator. He invented the face mask, employed a messenger guard system for sending in plays, tried to put audio devices in the helmets of his quarterbacks (almost *forty* years before pro football utilized this idea), used the flanker position by splitting the halfback from the backfield, and devised the draw play to slow down the rush of the defense.

Eventually, the competitors would copy every formula of Paul's system for success.

Paul Brown's success as a coach resulted from 1) his ability to recognize and acquire quality football players and assistant coaches; 2) his intense personal drive to win; 3) his complete control of the football program as both head coach and general manager; and 4) his emphasis on preparation and fundamentals.

Regarding the last point, each year in training camp Paul Brown distributed notebooks to his players. Everything we needed to learn, from the basic plays to the last play of the season, appeared on those pages. We'd write down the fundamentals of blocking, the fundamentals of the head-on tackle and side-tackle, the shoulder block, how to hit the blocking machine, how to do calisthenics, etc. All those fundamentals that you think kids had learned in high school—we had to practice every year.

Everyone had the same playbook, and every player had to memorize all the plays and positions, not just the plays which affected his own assignments. No one ever lost his playbook, although some of the guys used to play tricks on one another and hide them. (You would pay a heavy fine if you lost your book.)

Paul demanded that we study the playbook, and he would occasionally give us tests. I know that Jim Brown has mentioned that many of us cheated on these tests, that some of us used crib sheets. That's probably true. Although, I can't remember that anyone was ever caught cheating. But in the process of filling out those crib sheets, many players learned the assorted formations and plays.

Also, we looked at movies of our respective positions. The offensive linemen, for instance, were graded on the basic fundamentals of a block-stance, approach, contact and follow through. Our "stance" should be constant all the time. Our "approach" was getting into a position to get into the block—between the ball and the guy that we

Paul Brown in the Classroom.
John Nash, Cleveland State University Archives

blocked. "Contact" was how we hit and how we made our move to put ourselves between the tackler and the ball carrier so that the defenseman didn't make the tackle. After awhile all this became habit.

We worked on tackling fundamentals. We'd make two side tackles on each other after running onto the field (in rain, snow, or shine); then we'd execute a head on tackle. So that no teammate would get hurt, we would lift the runner and set him on his feet rather than on his back. We would also avoid tackling our teammate from behind.

After calisthenics we'd we'd hit the blocking machine. Then we'd discuss the philosophy of the play and how we should execute our blocks in regards to where the ball was going.

And then we started practicing the most simple running plays. Afterwards, passing plays were added into the format.

Later we would split into our own groups; the offensive line would practice separately, as would the defense. At the end of practice we would always conduct a "two-hand" scrimmage, where everything was full steam, but you wouldn't tackle.

Practice and game film would provide the coaching staff with concrete material on which to evaluate each player's performance. When the season was over each player would receive a grade which reflected the quality of performance on those plays in which he participated. A player's strengths and weaknesses were then disclosed. A tackle might hear, for example: "You were making good contact, but you weren't following through." So when you went to training camp the next year you worked on that weakness. Utilizing the film medium

Blocks like these (this particular one to help Dub Jones cross the goal line in our undefeated 1948 season) earned me six All-Pro honors at offensive tackle. I wore #46 until the Browns second year in the NFL; Marion Motley donned #76 before me.
Herman Seid, Cleveland State University Archives

to improve performance distinguished Paul Brown from his contemporaries. He was a perfectionist; he paid close attention to detail.

When the regular season began Paul altered the practice schedule. The schedule was always the same; consistency was one of Paul Brown's benchmarks as a coach. We'd play on Sunday, be off on Monday and Tuesday, and then concentrate on the offensive side of the ball on Wednesday. We were on the field about an hour and forty-five minutes. Thursdays were basically the same but with more attention given to the defense. On Friday we would practice for an hour. On Saturday we spent about thirty minutes, without wearing equipment, just running through the plays.

At Hiram wives and children would visit practice once in a while to watch. But the women would hide behind umbrellas and sneak around because they were not encouraged to attend practices. Practice was strictly business.

Paul emphasized preparation and execution over conditioning during the week before a game. He didn't want us to exhaust our energy before the game. He desired a fresh squad on Sundays. Speaking of saving up our strength, this brings to mind Paul's famous "Tuesday Rule" for married players. (Marital relations should be avoided from Tuesday until after Sunday's game.) I can't tell you if anyone really took Paul's Tuesday Rule seriously.

We'd stay at the Hotel Carter the night before home games. We'd always have dinner together and then we'd see a movie. Our wives were allowed to attend the movies with us, but then they had to return home. They couldn't stay with us overnight. Some of the players would visit the drugstore at the hotel and drink hot chocolate with their wives until it was time to head to our rooms for bed check.

There were 10:00 PM bed checks on the evenings before a game, whether we were home or away. His assistant coaches would check, not Paul.

We'd also have a team dinner party at the Hotel Cleveland every Sunday after the game. The dinner was for players, families, and friends. We had a great time together.

We were winning, so we didn't mind what we were asked to do. We accepted Paul's rules. Paul Brown believed that a college prospect's character was as important as was his ability, so Paul drafted players who were not going to be poor role models or a challenge to his authority. He expected excellent personal conduct from his players. At the beginning of each season as head coach of the Cleveland Browns, 1946-1962, he always mentioned in his opening speech to his team that "players who womanized or lived recklessly" would not be around long.

He established many rules, and there were no exceptions. For example, only clean T-shirts could be worn in camp, and at evening meal a dress shirt was required. And players had to always wear jackets and ties when appearing in public. Smoking was strictly prohibited in both the locker room and dining hall. "If you have to smoke," Paul stated, "don't smoke in public." Paul Brown didn't smoke himself.

He also discouraged drinking. If Paul drank, he never drank where someone would see him. I never knew of anybody who said they saw him take a drink. A few guys, however, continued to drink (privately, of course), but Paul didn't want to hear about it. I remember Paul going to a hotel on Cedar Road in Cleveland one night for dinner when the doorman said that one of his players was there. Paul turned around and left because he didn't want to catch the guy cheating on the rules.

Paul Brown kicked our tackle and captain off of the team after he was charged with intoxication by Cleveland Police. Even though the player was cleared of the intoxication charge and accepted a disorderly-conduct charge, Paul Brown refused to reinstate him.

Besides instilling fear (or respect for his absolute authority) into his players, Paul Brown motivated us by making us believe that we could become the "New York Yankees of Football." His goal was to make the Cleveland Browns such a powerhouse that people across the country would think "Cleveland Browns" when the topic of football entered into the conversation. He accomplished this goal.

Paul Brown's system worked. In the four years the Browns played in the All-America Football Conference we won all four championships. We defeated the New York Yankees (twice), the Buffalo Bisons, and the San Francisco 49ers in the title games. Our regular season record stood at an astounding 47-4-3, including an undefeated season in 1948 when we went 14-0. In our very first game in 1946 we crushed the Miami Seahawks, 44-0, and I kicked three field goals and five extra points. Our team once went 29 consecutive games without a loss. In that first year I led the league in scoring by tallying 84 points. I kicked 45 extra points and 13 field goals, breaking the existing NFL records in each category.

Look at the record of the Browns between 1946 and 1955. No team in professional football history dominated the game as did the Browns of this era. In those first ten years we appeared in ten consecutive championship games and won seven, including four AAFC and three NFL championships. In those ten years we won 105, lost 18 and tied 4 times in the regular season for a winning percentage of 83 percent.

We were drawing the largest crowds in the AAFC and in all of football as well. But near the end of our four years in the AAFC, our ascendancy to the top brought fewer and fewer fans to the lakefront. Our crowds began to show some apathy. Winning came too easily.

It was not difficult, however, getting up for an opponent despite our dominance. The credit goes to Paul Brown. This was a major trait of Paul Brown's success. He would motivate you while game film was being reviewed. He'd tell you in front of everyone what you might have done wrong. You didn't want to get your name mentioned. You were afraid if your name was mentioned too many times that you would not be around long. Paul's methods, although not always popular with the players, shaped a winning football team, and when you're winning, the game becomes fun. The Browns developed a winning attitude and, subsequently, wonderful esprit de corps. We were a family.

He was the boss (ruler and dictator) and everyone knew it. He coached and handled contract negotiations. Owner Arthur McBride had given Paul complete control of the organization. Paul picked the coaches and players that he wanted to work for him, and Paul decided what to pay them.

I recall Otto Graham saying that there were no prima donnas on the team. That's true. Take Jim Brown, for instance, who was perceived by some to pose a threat to Paul's authority. The fact is that Jim followed the rules like everyone else and never gave anything but his very best effort for Paul.

Many years later, at a golf outing named "Paul's Guys" in Dayton, Jim Brown was one of the first ex-Browns to arrive. Jim expressed to everyone how Paul Brown had inspired him as a football player by designing his entire offense around the great fullback. Jim and the rest of us often didn't realize how exceptional a coach Paul had been until after our playing years ended.

Paul was like any successful businessman. He developed and organizational strategy and then assigned a variety of responsibilities to his coaches to accomplish those objectives. Paul's coaches, like his players, were under a great deal of pressure because of Paul's obsession to control and win. He demanded perfection. Paul would never criticize a coach in front of the players, but I'm sure that he would "constructively criticize" his coaches in private.

Players got closer to Paul after retirement. I always got along well with him. "If you can't do the job, then, we'll find someone who can" seemed to be Paul Brown's motto. He might tell you that "you're making mistakes" or that "you're killing our football team."

He didn't give inspirational pep talks like former coach George Allen. At halftime, Blanton Collier, an assistant coach, would chart down on the blackboard the plays that we needed to run in the second half. He'd also talk about adjustments that we needed to make, plays that are working, etc. The players would also give input as to what plays, schemes, and formations might be successful. And the coach would write down the play that you suggested and you'd run that in the second half, if the coach agreed. So Paul wouldn't come into the locker room and inspire you with a "Let's win one for the Gipper" speech. Instead, he would summarize the first half and then discuss rationally what we could do in the second half to improve.

Paul could also "inspire" a player to quickly sign a proposed contract.

Here I am with Paul Brown—the greatest coach in football history.

At Ohio State, during the off-season, I roomed with Lin Houston, Dante Lavelli, and a friend named Bill Larkin from Martins Ferry. (A few years earlier Bill drove a milk truck for a summer job. On one trip Bill pulled off the side of the road and began transferring the empty bottles of milk from the top to the bottom, stacking the full bottles on top. As he worked in the back of his truck, a drunk driver skidded off the side of the road and smashed into him, taking off his leg. Wearing an artificial leg, Bill became an outstanding Industrial Arts teacher. I learned from Bill how to put my injuries in perspective.)

During one off-season Paul sent me a contract to my Ohio State address. This time I decided I'd wait a little bit longer to return the signed contract in order to squeeze a little more out of him. (He was perceived by some as being tight with the buck.) So I sent the contract back—unsigned. I didn't even include a note of explanation.

About a week later, I came up to play a basketball game in Cleveland. (We used to have a Cleveland Browns basketball team in the off-season. We got paid fifty dollars a game. Dante Lavelli, Otto Graham, Marion Motley, and other Browns played. We traveled all over Ohio and played pick-up teams. We had a lot of fun playing competitive basketball, and it was another way of keeping in shape.) Paul left word that he wanted to talk to me before I returned to Columbus. So I stopped in his office and he calmly asked, "So you don't plan on playing this year?"

I answered (defensively), "Sure, I plan on playing this year."

Paul then stated, "Well, you sent your contract back unsigned and you didn't say anything."

I then told Paul that I needed more money. And he proceeded to list all kinds of reasons why he couldn't give me a penny more. The fact that I requested more money didn't upset him as much as did my approach during the negotiation process. He took my actions personally, and I did feel twinges of guilt and betrayal with the way I behaved. From that point on, I learned a valuable lesson. If I had any problems with Paul about money or anything else, then I talked to him directly. I also learned not to talk to anyone else regarding any conflicts that I might have had with him.

Paul wanted no public discussions of salaries. No player knew what anyone else on the team made. Paul didn't want the wives sitting together at the games talking about their husbands' salaries. In those days you weren't in a good bargaining position. There were no player agents, and Paul would never have talked to an agent. You negotiated your own contract. Basically, you wanted to play. And you certainly never complained to the media about Paul's unwillingness to pay you more money or about anything else which happened behind closed doors. That would be suicidal. And when the AAFC collapsed after the 1949 season, the NFL and the Canadian Football League (CFL) were the only places of employment for football players. Paul said that he was the highest paid guy in the organization, and if anything had to be said to the media, he would be the one to say it.

* * *

Coach Brown utilized the kicking game like no other coach had done. Because I had the ability to kick a field goal from over 50 yards and because of my accuracy from anywhere inside the 50, Paul Brown possessed an offensive weapon which no other team at that time (or before) had owned. (Remember, a missed field goal in those days was sometimes as good as a punt. For instance, if my errant field goal landed in the end zone, then the other team would have possession at their twenty yard line.) Most offenses who just crossed midfield could only entertain two possibilities on fourth and short: go for the first down or punt. Paul, unlike his competition, had a third choice—I could kick a field goal and give us some points. And, as it turned out, those field goals often translated into Browns victories.

The Browns also benefited from my kickoffs which usually soared long and deep and into or near the end zone. (My strategy on a kick-off was always the same—to try to kick the ball out of the end zone so that it could not be returned.) This feature of the kicking game provided the Browns with great field position because our stingy de-fense often forced the opposition to punt from deep in their own ter-ritory.

Paul Brown directed me to kick field goals to a greater degree than anyone had before, and because I was regularly either breaking or es-tablishing new placekicking records, I soon captured the attention of fans and sportswriters. One local writer, James E. Doyle of the Cleveland *Plain Dealer,* originated my enduring nickname ("The Toe") in 1946, our first year. Doyle first tried the rhyme "Lou the Toza" with "Groza". Then he compressed this expression to "The Toe."

I got along wonderfully with the media, particularly with the Browns play-by-play announcer for many years, Ken Coleman. Gib Shanley replaced Ken Coleman when Ken moved back home to Bos-ton, and we also got along well. Gib was from Shadyside, near Mar-tins Ferry. I always kidded Gib about Shadyside being a suburb of Martins Ferry. Cleveland had some terrific broadcasters and sports-writers during my playing days—Jim Graner, Bob Neal, Whitey Lewis, Gordon Cobbledick, Chuck Heaton, Bob August, Frank Gibbons, Hal Lebovitz, Herman Goldstein, Bob Yonkers, and Regis McAuley, just to name a few.

Before kicking an extra point or a field goal, I used to extend my arms and plant my right foot under my right hand and drag my cleats in the turf to draw a line. The line pointed toward the center of the goalposts and insured proper alignment. Consistency is the hallmark of success in kicking, and I wanted every kick to be the same.

This procedure, however, required more time than was offered in a game situation. Don Greenwood, my first holder, suggested that I get a piece of adhesive tape and lay it down in place of the earlier, cleat-dragged line. Don's tip seemed like a good idea. For the next four years, before each kick I pulled from my helmet a 72-inch rolled piece of adhesive tape. (I took two sticky sides of one-inch adhesive tape and stuck them together, one on top, one on the bottom, creating one long strip). This ritual received enough attention to warrant an article and photographs in America's most popular magazine, *Life*. I employed this tape until our first year in the NFL. The NFL ruled the tape illegal because it was a "theatrical device," whatever that meant.

Stretched along the ground is a strip of adhesive tape which guided my early placekicks.

Sometimes training camp provided good theater. Chubby Grigg, a big tackle who played with us from 1948-1951, was a real character. At Bowling Green we didn't have any air conditioning; we only had electric fans. And Chubby used to slip inside these pink bloomers and walk around the dormitories in them. He weighed over 300 pounds. When training camp broke we usually played an exhibition game at the Akron Rubber Bowl. An assistant coach was standing in the lobby of an Akron hotel while Chubby got one of those big horse blanket pins and hid it in his bloomers. The coach was standing with his hands in his pockets, and his coat was all bunched. So Chubby sneaked up behind him and pinned the bloomers to his coat. Everybody was laughing and the coach couldn't figure out that we were laughing at him.

The Browns moved the training camp from Bowling Green to Hiram in 1951. I enjoyed the facilities at Bowling Green, but I preferred Hiram College because it was nearer to my home in Berea.

At Hiram Paul kept us busy. We practiced twice a day. And the only time we had any free time was right after practice, just before dinner. I could go and meet Jackie somewhere at that time. I remember Jackie and I, along with teammate Don Colo and his wife, enjoyed an early evening picnic off the training camp grounds and proceeded to get lost in some park. Darkness approached and we needed to hurry back to training camp to avoid breaking curfew. We were frantic. Somehow we found the right country road which took us back to Hiram just in time.

Equipment manager Morrie Kono began a tradition at Hiram known as the "Turkey Hunt." Morrie informed the rookies on the first day of training camp each year that a large, fresh, delectable turkey would be theirs for a future meal if they carefully followed a map and a series of cryptic instructions. In reality, though, there was neither a secret destination nor a turkey to be discovered. Morrie would randomly pick an address out of the phonebook, miles away in the country, and the directions led these amateur sleuths to a one very embarrassing find—no turkey and some bewildered expressions on the faces of some confused homeowners. Some rookies detected Morrie's insidious plans before they got in their cars and drove off in search of the turkey treasure, but more than a few rookies fell for this joke to the delight of Morrie and the veterans.

Once Morrie hid Tommy Flynn, another equipment manager, in a storage trunk. Our end Horace Gillom reached in the trunk to pull out a clean jersey when Flynn jumped out at him. Horace about dropped to the floor in shock.

Morrie's wry sense of humor would enliven my days with the Browns for many years.

Leo Murphy, our trainer, was always "one of the guys" despite not being a player. Leo provided us with music (piano) and with a lot of laughs through the years. He and Morrie made a great team and they added to the family atmosphere which contributed to the Browns success.

Although he was more visible to the players when the regular season began, our owner Arthur McBride would sometimes visit his team at camp. And occasionally we'd see Arthur at practice or in the locker room before or after a game. But basically he stayed in the background and allowed Paul to run the program. Paul Brown had complete control of the team. Paul was lucky to have this; it was an ideal situation for him. I don't know how they got along personally, but professionally it seemed a perfect match.

Arthur McBride was often called Mickey. He was a self-made millionaire and owned a local cab company plus a lot of real estate on Cleveland's far west side. He was very friendly and enthusiastic.

Owner McBride became famous for inventing (with Paul Brown's assistance) the "taxi squad." In those days football teams could carry thirty-three players on their rosters. The Browns had some athletes who the coaches thought would develop into roster players but who needed some more seasoning, more practice and experience. Reluctant to release these certain players because of the risk of other teams snatching them, the Browns carried about five extra players on "the cab squad" or "taxi squad." They were technically on Mickey McBride's cab company's payroll (even though they never once got behind the wheel of a yellow cab) instead of the payroll of the Browns. That's how the expression ("cab squad" or "taxi squad" originated). These "cabbies" would practice everyday with the regulars but not dress during game time. Some members of the cab squad did make the actual roster.

McBride was the owner from 1946 until Dave Jones, a Cleveland industrialist, bought the club in 1953 for $600,000. Art Modell followed Dave Jones as principal owner in 1961.

Longtime assistant coach Blanton Collier replaced Paul Brown as head coach of the Browns amid much controversy in 1963. Paul was fired by Art Modell during a local newspaper strike which added to the drama. I remember Blanton calling me and asking for some advice. He knew that I was close to Paul, and Blanton had some very strong reservations about taking over the position from the guy who hired him many years ago and who was also his friend and mentor. I told Blanton that he should take the position because Paul would want him to be his successor. Blanton, as decent and kind and capable a coach as you could find, after much thought agreed to become the second head coach in Browns history.

Prior to World War II Blanton had been a high school coach in Paris, Kentucky. He was at Great Lakes Naval Training Station as a seaman when Paul Brown was the head coach. Paul Brown noticed a man who came to every practice and who busied himself with taking down notes. Paul thought that this guy might have been a scout or something. Impressed with this man's attentiveness and eagerness, Paul found out that Blanton was a high school coach, so he put him on his staff. And that began a relationship that lasted a long time. Blanton was the defensive coordinator at first. Later Blanton became the offensive coordinator, so he understood both sides of the line. A brilliant tactician, in the off-season he took the game film (movies) home with him and graded us as to how well we did in our particular positions.

When training camp opened in 1963, there wasn't any noticeable difference between Collier's camp and Paul's. The format was essentially the same. The transition from Paul to Blanton went smoothly. The Browns continued to be a potent franchise, and in 1964, Blanton's second year, the Browns would become champions for the only time during Art Modell's reign, and for the eighth and last time in my twenty-one years of service.

*   *   *

My brother Alex played several basketball games for Kentucky at the National Invitational Tournament (NIT) in New York City during spring break in 1948 and 1949. At the time Alex knew a girl by the name of Jackie Lou Robbins, who was from Martins Ferry. Five years younger than me, Jackie was in junior high when I was in high school. She was a popular radio personality for a time at WWVA in Wheeling and had just graduated from high school and had gone to New York to model. But I didn't know her personally because of our age difference. I knew about Jackie from a radio show called "Wheeling Steel Hour" where she performed.

Jackie went with her dance teacher to New York City in 1947 after graduating from high school. Jackie worked as a designer's model in New York City from the summer of 1947 until 1949.

The first time that I saw Jackie was at Ebbets Field when we played the Brooklyn Dodgers of the All-America Football Conference. After the game we were introduced. She arrived at the ballpark with this young musician from Martins Ferry.

Our first date happened solely by chance. I went to New York in 1948 with my ATO fraternity brothers to watch Alex play in the NIT. During this visit Alex asked me to take his place at a dinner date with Jackie because he had caught the flu bug. Remembering who she was (from Ebbets Field), I agreed (without much arm twisting) to be a substitute for my brother. Agreeing to this date was the best decision I made in my life. I fell in love with her right on the spot. We've been "dating" ever since—we've been married for forty-five years.

We were married in Martins Ferry on May 13, 1950. Jackie is not Catholic and I was, and at that time you couldn't be married in the Catholic church if both partners were not Catholic. Fr. Connelly performed the morning (9:30) ceremony at the St. Mary's rectory. Jackie and I had a small family wedding and afterwards enjoyed our wedding breakfast at the McClure Hotel in Wheeling.

We quickly departed for a month-long honeymoon. That first weekend was spent in Washington, PA, and then we started driving south and stayed a week at The Cloister at Sea Island. We also visited Myrtle Beach. We took our time and stopped when we felt like it and eventually made it to Florida.

When we returned home we noticed a note on our apartment door saying to call our good friends the Rymkuses. Lou Rymkus and his wife Bette had been like parents to us. We called them only to find out that my father had died that very same day of our return, June 13, exactly a month after we were married. The death was not sudden. Dad was, in fact, too sick to attend our wedding. He was in the hospital when Jackie and I exchanged vows.

* * *

The All-America Football Conference devised a curious numbering system to distinguish itself from the NFL.   In 1946 the AAFC required that the centers wear numbers in the #20s; guards, #30s; tackles, #40s; ends, #50s; quarterbacks, #60s; fullbacks, #70s; halfbacks, #80s and 90s. In our second season in the NFL (1951) we conformed to the NFL system: centers, #50s; guards, #60s; tackles, #70s; ends, #80s; quarterback, #teens; fullbacks, #30s; halfbacks, #20s. I wore #46, since I was a tackle, and I didn't inherit my more famous #76, the number the Browns later retired, until we moved into the NFL. Marion Motley wore #76 before me.   More importantly, the rules of the game of football were identical between the two leagues.

The league was divided into two divisions—the Eastern (Brooklyn Dodgers, Buffalo Bisons, Miami Seahawks, and New York Yankees) and the Western (Chicago Rockets, Cleveland Browns, Los Angeles Dons, and San Francisco 49ers). I spoke of our supremacy already. Our team's success probably was a major reason why the AAFC folded. Fans were not interested in watching their teams get hammered by the Browns. We easily outdrew the other AAFC franchises, but even our loyal fans grew apathetic. Those consistently record-sized football crowds that many associate with Cleveland Browns football didn't start until we joined the NFL.

In 1950 the Baltimore Colts, Cleveland Browns, and San Francisco 49ers became members of the NFL. The rest of the players from the defunct AAFC were placed in a pool and selected by NFL teams.

Despite our four consecutive championships, we only heard from the detractors who claimed that we won in an inferior league. These commentators, mostly NFL players and coaches, believed (and secretly hoped) that the Browns would get roughed up in the NFL. We were taunted with expressions like "Go get a football."

George Marshall, owner of the NFL Washington Redskins, declared that the NFL's "weakest team could toy with us." Legendary Bears coach George Halas believed that the Browns did not stand a chance of winning many games in the NFL. His attitude may have been altered, however, after we defeated his team in a pre-season game that first year.

But the regular season, some thought, would prove Halas right. Our first NFL opponent would surely determine if we were ready to play with the "big boys." We were matched against the defending NFL champions, the Philadelphia Eagles, at their own stadium. Greasy Neale, the Eagles head coach, derisively stated that "Cleveland was just a basketball team. All they can do is throw."

Neale and his overconfident Eagles, along with 71,237 fans in Philadelphia's Municipal Stadium, soon learned who was pro football's best team. Otto Graham threw touchdown passes to Dub Jones, Mac Speedie, and Dante Lavelli. And Graham and Rex Bumgardner ran for the other two scores as we humbled the Eagles (and the rest of the NFL) 35-10.

I bruised my left shoulder while throwing a block on a punt return, the first time we had the ball, and I had to watch from the sidelines. My replacement, Chubby Grigg successfully booted five extra points.

I remember that after the game the NFL Commissioner, Bert Bell, visited our locker room and told us that we were "the best football football team that I (Bert Bell) have ever seen."

Coach Brown, however, wisely muted Bell's compliment and his team's enthusiasm by saying, "We are not going to gloat over this victory. There is a long season ahead." But the win over Philadelphia provided the impetus to go 10-2 that first year in the NFL, and the confidence needed to win two post-season games.

To get to the NFL title game we had to get by conference-rival New York, who also owned a 10-2 mark. The Giants had given us our only two defeats, by the scores of 6-0 and 17-13, so they had a psychological edge. Their ingenious coach, Steve Owens, developed an "umbrella defense" which effectively thwarted our vaunted passing attack.

For the conference playoff, all the players on both teams wore sneakers because of the icy turf at Cleveland Municipal Stadium. In these near-zero temperatures, I wore a sneaker on my left foot and a football shoe without the cleats on my right foot. I broke a 3-3 tie with a 29-yard field goal in the last 58 seconds of the game to give us the win. I was carried off the field by my teammates.

But an even bigger play was made earlier by middle guard Bill Willis when he chased down Giants speedster Choo Choo Roberts on the four-yard line. Roberts had 47 yards of open field to cross for the winning touchdown. Incredibly, though, Willis finally caught up with Choo Choo and tackled him from behind.

I couldn't have imagined that the 1950 season would yet provide an even more thrilling conclusion.

Ironically, the former Cleveland Rams, now the Los Angeles Rams, would battle the Cleveland Browns for the 1950 NFL title at Cleveland Municipal Stadium, where the Rams had won the NFL championship in 1945 over the Washington Redskins, 15-14, in bitter cold conditions.

The game would match the league's best offense (the Rams) vs. the league's best defense (the Browns). In twelve games the Rams averaged nearly 40 points a contest, while our defense allowed an average of 12 points per game. Norm Van Brocklin, Bob Waterfield, Tom Fears, and Elroy Hirsch were the future Hall-of-Famers who led the attack for the Rams. Fears, in fact, had caught 84 passes that year.

For the championship game (on Christmas Eve) against the Rams the field was again frozen as it was the previous week against the Giants. The game swung back and forth, and with three minutes remaining in the fourth quarter we were down 28-27. We missed an extra point in the first half when a snap sailed away from my holder, Tommy James. Tommy picked up the ball and tried to throw a pass, but the toss went incomplete.

Otto Graham marched us into field goal range (near the thirty-yard line) but fumbled away the ball as he stretched for extra yardage and was blindsided. I remember Paul Brown putting his arm around Otto's shoulder as our dejected quarterback walked to the sidelines. I heard Paul say to Otto, "Don't worry. We'll get it back. We'll win this thing yet."

Our defense stopped the Rams in three plays. Had they converted a first down, the game would have been over. Cliff Lewis carried the punted ball to our 32-yard line after catching it on the 19. One minute and 50 seconds remained.

In the most dramatic last-minute football drive I've ever seen or participated in, Graham rushed and passed our offense to the 9-yard line of the Rams with 28 seconds left. Now it was my turn.

Otto left the field of play as the field-goal unit stepped in. Despite the obvious significance of the kick, I wasn't nervous. I didn't have time to think about it.

I retreated from my tackle position. Nothing was different—I lined up as I did on any other field-goal effort. I was kicking toward the bleachers, the open end of the stadium, where a right-to-left cross-wind was whipping across the frozen turf. If I struck the ball properly, then the wind would not be a factor from this distance.

As I had done on all of my field goals, in my mind I focused on my checklist: stance and approach, contact, and follow-through.

Frank Gatski snapped the ball cleanly to Tommy James who precisely set it down. The protection from the guys up front was excellent. Everything advanced like clockwork. I struck the ball solidly and instantly realized that the ball would easily sail over the crossbar and between the uprights.

Before the referee signaled that the kick was good, Tommy James leaped in joy as he watched the flight of the ball. The football soared straight and true as the rest of my teammates joined Tommy in the celebration.

Warren Lahr intercepted a long pass thrown by Van Brocklin a few moments later to secure the win and ignite a frenzied jubilation. Fans streamed onto the field, and one reveler tried to rip off my jersey, almost choking me in the process.

After I flipped this young man over my shoulder and sprinted toward the dugout which led to the locker room tunnel, I noticed near the steps that Paul Brown had suddenly stopped and was bent over, hyperventilating, trying to catch his breath and attempting to gather his composure.

Pandemonium engulfed our locker room as players shouted and laughed in complete abandonment. Reporters and photographers converged on the players and coaches as we hugged each other. I had removed my kicking shoe and some of my teammates (and even owner Mickey McBride) raised the shoe in tribute before kissing it. This particular shoe was later bronzed by my good friend Harry Leitch, and even the Smithsonian Museum in Washington D. C. displays one of my kicking shoes.

My biggest field goal, the 16-yarder in the closing seconds against the Rams, giving us our first NFL championship (in 1950).
Cleveland State University Archives

Paul Brown spoke only briefly to us, telling us how proud he was of our performance. Commissioner Bert Bell visited our dressing room and announced that we were "the greatest team ever to play football."

What a thrill—our first year in the NFL and most NFL players and fans were telling us during the previous four years that we were minor leaguers. We felt vindicated. We proved that we could win in the NFL. And, personally, to have a chance to win a championship with a last-second field goal was something placekickers usually only dream about. All those years of practice and hard work made this miracle come true for me.

There was no downtown parade in Cleveland following our historic triumph because Christmas Day would be tomorrow. Jackie and I drove to Columbus, where Jackie's folks lived. The full and satisfying realization of our win over the Rams didn't sink in until we got to Columbus.

From Columbus we went down to Martins Ferry, and the fire department took me for a ride on a fire truck through town, just as they did when my high school team had captured the state basketball championship nine years ago.

* * *

Father Connelly was our parish priest at St. Mary Catholic Church in Martins Ferry when I was in high school. Fr. Connelly would often watch the Martins Ferry sports teams practice. Father wondered why he didn't see me in church. Out of respect for this kind and gentle man, I started going to church regularly, and we became close friends.

I remember at the state basketball tournament, in a district game in front of a full house at Steubenville, our Protestant coach asked Fr. Connelly to come over and sit on our bench. Father said at a banquet later that he knew we were going to win that game because we had a priest on our bench and Steubenville Catholic, our opponent that night, didn't. Father Connelly would continue the tradition of joining the Martins Ferry athletes on the playing field (or court, diamond, etc.) for many years.

Surrounding the beloved Father Connelly are (left to right) Bill Young, Alex Groza, me, and Jack McCarty.

Father Connelly served as a military priest in Casablanca in the African Campaign during World War II. When the war was over and I became a professional football player, Fr. Connelly worked at Lancaster Industrial School, a boys school (or reform school) for delinquents and incorrigibles. While I was pursuing my degree in marketing from Ohio State in the off-season, I occasionally visited Father Connelly in nearby Lancaster.

At the school I talked with some of the kids and played Ping-Pong with some of them. I developed a friendly relationship with a few of the boys in the hope of providing some guidance and direction in their lives. I remember one boy, a real affable kid. When I returned to Lancaster on a subsequent visit, this youngster apparently had seemed ready for society and had been released. I asked Fr. Connelly about this young man and how he was getting along in the outside world. Fr. Connelly told me that boy had just returned to Lancaster Industrial School. I asked Father, why? And Fr. Connelly said that the boy's environment at Lancaster was better than it was in his neighborhood. So the young man intentionally went out and stole a car to get back into the school.

Fr. Connelly used to drive up to Detroit during the summers, and Bowling Green, the Browns first training camp, was on his route. He'd always stop and see me at Bowling Green where we'd be practicing. The first time he stopped at Bowling Green was on a hot summer's day, and he had taken off his collar and black priest's shirt. He placed these items on the seat beside him. He wore only a t-shirt.

At camp he immediately recognized Paul Brown and asked him, "Where can I find Lou Groza?"

Paul snapped, "Who the hell wants to see him? Who the heck are you?"

Then Fr. Connelly calmly introduced himself to a startled and chagrined Paul Brown who had only just now noticed the priestly attire on the seat next to Father. Paul was won over immediately by Fr. Connelly's warmth and politeness. They soon became friends, and Fr. Connelly became the Browns chaplain.

My faith in God has comforted me through a lot of tough times. And I credit my relationship with Fr. Connelly for turning me around spiritually. He passed away about ten years ago. Fr. Connelly's housekeeper told me that in his last moments before his death, Father asked her to "Thank Lou Groza for me."

* * *

To be successful at kicking (or at anything else) you must understand and apply the fundamentals. I learned a lot from my brother Frank. He showed me the basic principal of finding the spot on the ball where to kick. That spot is right below the center of the football. You hold your heel down, and you jam your foot through the ball, so that when your toe hits the ball, the toe projects up through the middle of the ball from below. In other words, the foot does not go through the ball on a straight line as you kick it.

The ball should be positioned vertically by the holder because this gives the ball more resistance, and the ball absorbs your foot more efficiently and powerfully. Pointing the laces forward also is important. Placing the laces toward the kicker affects accuracy because a kicker's vision is disrupted when the laces are conspicuous. And a kicker hits the ball more solidly when the laces are placed toward the goalposts.

To repeat, you should kick the ball just under center. In a geometric sense, then, you are drawing a plane at the angle that rises through the middle of the football, coming from under the center of the ball, that goes through the ball. You're trying to protect your foot from straying from the parameters of this imagined plane. And with your heel down the ball is struck and then lifted with the power of kicking the football directly through the middle. Your kicking foot should now land in front of the spot where the ball was kicked for your follow-through.

And this is what I used to practice all the time, whether it was an extra point or field goal. I kicked every kick the same way because I didn't want to develop any bad habits. Starting with my right foot, I would take two steps—one short and then one long, culminating in a long, lunging step into the ball. I used to work on fundamentals—stance approach, contact, and follow-through. And when I was having any difficulty I'd work in practice on finding out what the problem was. (Usually, my problem was that I would get too close to the football in my approach to the ball.) My left foot always came down about six inches behind the ball. Because my momentum was driving through the ball all the time, rather than hitting it and falling back, I was hitting it and going through it.

In practice I kicked field goals of over sixty yards. My longest field goal sailed 52 yards in a loss at home against the New York Giants in 1952. I possessed a strong leg (in 1957, for instance, I kicked 5 field goals over 50 yards), but I was more concerned with accuracy than distance. In 1953, for example, I made 23 field goals in 26 attempts (88.5 %). This was accomplished while I blocked as a starting offensive tackle and long before the centering of the hash marks and emergence of artificial turf, two developments which greatly benefited the modern placekicker.

I have a few remarks to make about the kicking shoe. The straight-ahead placekickers of my generation always kicked with a specially designed shoe with a hard-leather-squared toe. (When the field was frozen I would I wear a tennis shoe—instead of a regular

Mastering the fundamentals of kicking took practice and concentration. *Cleveland Browns*

football shoe—on my left foot for better traction.) I had worn a kicking shoe in high school and college. Today's soccer-style booters don't employ a specifically designed shoe because they don't kick with the toe as I did. My kicking shoe was a size 11D, one size smaller than my regular shoe size. The snugness prevented any slippage. Sports manufacturers attempted to enhance the productivity of kickers by putting weights in the toe and wedges in the sole. I didn't wear a weighted shoe.

The role of the holder is an underrated, yet critical element in a successful kicking game. I was fortunate to work with a talented group. Don Greenwood, the one who suggested I use a tape to line up my kicks, was my first holder from 1946-1947. Tommy James, my teammate at Ohio State, replaced Don in 1948 and held for me through 1955, the longest of anyone. Jim Ninowski and Bobby Franklin held the ball for me in later years. (When Ninowski was holding for me, once, I remember, I missed a 35-yard field goal. I just hadn't made solid contact. I came off the field and I wasn't aware of it, but Paul Brown was asking Jim Ninowski what he—Jim— was doing wrong. "What happened?" Jim and I have laughed about this incident many times.) Franklin and Tommy James were my favorites because they were adept at getting the ball down quickly and pointing the laces forward.

Frank Gatski snapped the ball to my holder from 1946-1956, and John Morrow and Fred Hoaglin centered for me in the 1960's.

As the kicking game improved in football, the extra-point became automatic after a while. The goalposts were on the goal line for a long time, so extra points were rarely missed. About the only time that you missed an extra point was when the blocking failed and a defenseman broke through the line, or when there was a bad snap, or when the snap was mishandled by the holder. One of my Browns records underscores the efficiency and predictability of converting the point-after- touchdown (PAT). From 1963 to 1966, I converted 138 consecutive PATS.

Moving the goalposts to the end line has increased the risk of missing PATS in today's game. And I'm also glad to see that pro football has given the team the two-point conversion option. Another recent rule change regarding kicking seems sensible.

We were kicking off from the 40 yard line in my day. Usually kick-offs went into the end zone and slowed the pace of the game for both players and fans. Today, kicking from the greater distance of the 30 yard line not only speeds up the contest but also adds more suspense. Now there is a better chance for a long return and better field position, which translates into more scoring opportunities and more action.

I suppose I brought more specialization to professional football. Since I only kicked when I returned to the Browns roster in 1961, other teams around the league began to hire players whose job was simply to placekick. When only thirty-three players completed a roster, you needed to have a kicker who could play another position. When roster sizes were expanded, specialization in the placekicking (and in many other areas of the game) set in. I didn't realize at the time how fortunate I was to be both a kicker and an offensive tackle. This flexibility gave me a better chance to make the Browns.

* * *

Injuries come with the territory of football, and in twenty-one years I have had my share.

In 1946 at Ebbets Field against the Brooklyn Dodgers, I damaged my lower back on a kickoff. After kicking the ball I ran downfield to tackle the ballcarrier, Lewis Mayne, who would be a Brown the next season. (In my early kicking days I didn't remain in the background, like today's kickers, and function as a safety valve. I always wanted to be the first guy down the field. I made many tackles on kickoffs. I was a football player.) To make the tackle I cut sharply and my cleats grabbed the turf. In stopping so suddenly, I incurred a double sprain of the left ankle.

My teammates didn't miss me much. We crushed the Dodgers, 66-14. However, the severity of the sprain put me in the hospital, and the Browns were concerned because the AAFC championship game against the tough New York Yankees was only two weeks away.

After recuperating for a week at Charity Hospital in Cleveland, I was ready to return to action. The trainers wrapped so much tape around my left ankle that I felt as if I were wearing a cast. I kicked two extra points and booted several deep kickoffs as we defeated the Yankees, 14-9, for the AAFC championship. In 1946 and 1947 I was just kicking. Paul didn't believe that I was ready to become a starting offensive tackle until my third year, 1948.

In our very first game against a NFL opponent, Philadelphia (in 1950), I hurt my shoulder and sat out the remainder of that historic game. On a punt return, I fell back with the other blockers to form a wedge. Don Phelps caught the ball and started to run behind our wall of blockers. I zeroed in on this one guy, but so did one of my teammates. I didn't see my teammates coming, and he smashed into my left shoulder. (Phelps proceeded to dash 64 yards for a touchdown, but the play was called back because of a clipping penalty.) Chubby Grigg did the kicking until I returned, and he kicked all five extra points. My shoulder bruise kept me out of action for the next several games. I came back and played but with my shoulder strapped.

I got hurt in a Friday night contest against the Chicago Bears. Gail Morrow, center John Morrow's wife, was staying with Jackie for the weekend. On Saturday morning a taxi carrying John and me pulled into my driveway. Jackie and Gayle came out to welcome us and noticed that both John and I had been roughed up the previous evening.

My jaw was wired because I got one tooth knocked out and had cracked a root in another tooth. My mouth advertised a swollen clump—one tooth was in the jaw and the other one was fractured at the root. The wire in my lower jaw held this clump together, and I wore that for a long time hoping that the injury would heal itself. Eventually the wire ended up breaking off, and I received orthodontic surgery.

John Morrow didn't feel very chipper either. John could barely walk as he tried to leave the taxi with Gail's assistance. He had hurt his back. We all laughed—football is a great bodybuilder.

Paul Brown invented the face mask, specifically a single plastic bar to protect his quarterback, Otto Graham, from breaking his jaw or nose and subsequently from missing playing time. Otto was our most valuable player, and he took a good deal of punishment and many cheap shots from his opponents.

The incident which provoked Paul Brown to design a special helmet for Otto occurred in a particularly rugged game against the 49ers in 1953. A rookie middle guard of the 49ers dove at an already sprawled Graham out of bounds and directly in front of our bench. His right elbow opened a cut on Otto's mouth large enough to require 15 stitches. Paul exploded with rage and the rest of the team committed themselves to avenging this attack on our leader. Otto bravely returned in the second half with renewed fury and also with a clear strip of plastic across the front of his helmet to inspire us to a 23-21 victory.

When Paul replaced the clear plastic strip with a bar—the face mask was born. The bar offered both protection and visibility for his quarterback and ultimately for football players everywhere. Prior to Otto's wearing a face mask, the only guys who would wear any facial protective device (cages) would be players who had broken their nose or cheekbone. Football equipment manufacturers began to incorporate Paul's idea into their helmets, and soon everybody started to wear masks.

The single-bar helmet ironically once contributed to one of my injuries. On kickoffs I would often get blindsided. Against Washington during a kickoff as I extended myself to tackle the ballcarrier, he cut and caught me in the face with his elbow, breaking the bar. The shattered bar then punctured my nose.

At halftime the trainers cleaned and patched the wound so that I could continue to play after the intermission. After the game and shower, I went into the training room to get some dressing on my nose, and my two little boys, Jeff and Jon, were in the locker room and watched the doctor stitch up my nose. Excited about seeing me getting sewn up, they didn't want to leave until the "surgery" ended. I saw facial abrasions and two black eyes when I glanced at a rearview mirror on my drive back to Berea that evening. A little later I pulled into the driveway, where my boys were anxiously awaiting my arrival. My kids reacted to my broken and cut nose with these words: "Boy, Dad, you really look neat!"

* * *

It's difficult to say which team was the most talented because I played on eight championship teams. If you look at our record while I was with the Browns (1946-1959, 1961-1967), you will see that we only had one season with a losing record. (In 1956 we won 5 and lost 7.) That's twenty winning seasons in twenty-one years. The Browns always seemed to have great players and great continuity from one year to the next. Paul's original team in 1946 provided the nucleus for many years. Paul also understood when it was time to replace the veteran with the rookie or to trade or draft to fill in any holes.

In our early years, the Cleveland Browns won all the time, so attendance dropped off in the AAFC. In our first six seasons we lost only eight times, so fans at home and away lost interest. We were winning practically all of the time.

If you saw Cleveland Stadium in the 1950 championship game, for example, then you noticed a lot of empty seats. The fact that the game was held on Christmas Eve during very cold temperatures certainly contributed to the dismal attendance figure. But this game was the most important game played by any Browns team in our brief history, and still only 29,751 spectators attended. Over the passage of time, attendance figures grew in Cleveland and throughout the entire NFL. In two more years, for example, over 50,000 fans watched us battle the Detroit Lions in the 1952 title game, which reflected the increasing popularity of professional football.

We didn't get many dollars ($500) for winning the first AAFC championship game in 1946 (or for winning the next three titles, for that matter). Instead of rings we received tie clasps. But the spoils which went to the victors increased as football's popularity grew when network television began broadcasting football games.

Team records are relative. Wins and losses are based on the talent of your team compared with the capabilities of your opponents. The Browns became a football dynasty largely because they had the most gifted athletes. But that excellence could not have been realized without superb leadership at all levels. We had the best coaches, the best scouts, in short, the best organization. Eventually, the other clubs in professional football, drawing from Paul Brown's winning formula, caught up to us. Today, the San Francisco 49ers are the Browns of another era. The reason for the success of the 49ers is simple—they have great talent and a superb organization.

The Detroit Lions were the toughest team for us to beat because they had outstanding players and fine coaches. Detroit's head coach, Buddy Parker, was the exact opposite of Paul Brown. Parker was loud and animated while Brown was quiet and introverted. Buddy Parker also did not create a lengthy list of rules for his players to follow. Paul Brown's demanded that his players not drink or smoke. And, of course, Detroit would take great delight out of Paul's restraints. Once in Akron after an exhibition game, Detroit's team bus was parked next to ours, and we could see many of their players drinking beer. As they consumed the beverage, the Lions smiled and mockingly toasted us as we soberly sat in Paul Brown's "dry" bus.

The leader of the Lions, of course, was quarterback Bobby Layne. Bobby enjoyed some drinks after a game, but his off-the-field reputation never seemed to affect the quality of his play. Featuring a beautiful touch, this Texan was one of the most gifted passers I have ever seen. He could also run the ball with quickness and without fear, and was very much like Otto in this respect. Bobby was a fiery competitor and had his team really behind him . Like the Browns, the Lions possessed excellent chemistry.

Detroit beat us in the title game in 1952, 17-7, and again in 1953, 17-16. (I kicked 3 field goals in the 1953 loss.) We thought that the better team in each contest had not won. We finally broke our unlucky streak against the Lions in 1954 when we avenged our previous championship losses by crushing them, 56-10. But in 1957 they humiliated us in the title game, 59-14. Before the 1957 slaughter we had lost two quarterbacks to injuries. And our leader, Otto Graham, had retired after the 1955 season.

On the subject of championship games, we defeated the New York Yankees,14-9, at home in the inaugural AAFC championship. We beat the Yankees again the next year, 14-3, in front of a big crowd (61,879) at Yankee Stadium. Our 49-7 over Buffalo in 1948 capped an undefeated season. (The 1972 Miami Dolphins are the only other professional team to have an unblemished record.) And we defeated the Bills in our final AAFC title contest, 31-21. After we nipped the Los Angeles Rams, 30-28, in perhaps the greatest professional football game ever played, the Rams got revenge and the NFL title in 1951 by the score of 24-17. Detroit beat us the next two years in two close championship games before our win over them in 1954. Otto's last game was a 38-14 championship victory at Los Angeles. The Lions defeated us for the title in 1957. And my eighth (and last) championship win came against Baltimore in 1964 when we shocked the highly-favored Colts, 27-0. (I also participated in three playoff games in 1950, 1958, and 1967, my last season.)

Except for three championship and two playoff losses, easily the most disheartening defeat came against the New York Giants in our last regular season game of 1958. A tie or a win would have given us the Eastern Division title and an appearance in the championship game. Late in the game we allowed the Giants to win the game, 13-10, with a 49-yard field goal by Pat Summerall. Summerall's kick was truly remarkable considering the fact that he had just missed badly from 36 yards. Added to this were the horrendous field conditions at the time Summerall kicked the ball. The field was completely covered in snow; snow was falling heavily; a brisk wind flew across the turf; and the footing was treacherous. Nonetheless, Summerall overcame all these conditions and booted the football cleanly between the uprights.

The following week we had to meet the Giants in a playoff game. They completely shut down our offense and beat us, 10-0. The Giants, however, lost in overtime the following week to the Colts in a historic championship encounter.

I had the honor of going to the Pro Bowl in Los Angeles nine times. In those days the players took those all-star games seriously and really tried to win the game for their respective conferences. We needed the extra dollars that came with playing in these games.

After the All-America Football Conference folded there still was one more game to be played—an all-star game in Houston called the Shamrock Bowl, near Houston's Shamrock Hotel. Glen McCarthy, an oil magnate, sponsored this game.

I remember that the all-stars attended a cocktail party before dinner. Our hosts were particularly gracious, and everyone seemed to be enjoying themselves. The guys from the opposing conference had an even better time because our coach for the game, Paul Brown, was at the party so naturally we couldn't drink, and we had to leave the party early so that we wouldn't break curfew (bed check). Paul's rules had to be followed even during all-star contests.

I played for a number of different coaches in various Pro Bowls. If I had not been a Brown I probably would have enjoyed playing for Vince Lombardi or Tom Landry. Vince and Paul were actually pretty close friends. Lombardi was an assistant coach with Jimmy Lee Howe for the Giants before he took over the head job at Green Bay. Lombardi used to ask me questions about how Paul ran his football team. Lombardi was humble (and smart) enough to pick up bits and pieces from different players from other teams about coaching styles. I also liked Tom Landry, the coach of the Cowboys. His demeanor was similar to Paul's—quiet, serious, and analytical. Like Paul Brown, Tom Landry was a winner.

One question which I get asked quite often centers on whether football players of my era were as good as today's stars. It's difficult to compare football players of different eras. I weighed 235 pounds when I first wore the brown and orange, and that was considered large for a football player. Today's players are much bigger. Linemen today typically weigh 300 pounds.

Also, players from my period generally did not vary as greatly in size as do today's athletes. There wasn't the huge difference in height and weight between players that you see now. In the 1940's and 1950's many lineman, in fact, were not much bigger than some of the backs. Yesterday's linemen might have been more mobile than today's linemen. Paul Brown use to check our speed in the 40-yard dash all the time, and I ran the 40 in 4.8 seconds. When the game went from a style dominated by the run to more passing, the size of the player came more into play. Pass protection necessitated taller and heavier lineman.

Players from my era, however, were tougher. I remember Larry Wilson, the Hall-of-Fame free safety of the St. Louis Cardinals, playing a game against us with two broken hands. It was my job to block two of the greatest defensive ends in the history of the game—Andy Robustelli and Doug Atkins. These guys would never let up, and they played with injuries which would keep today's players on the side-lines.

I also bumped heads against some great defensive tackles who played rough but clean football—Ernie Stautner, Al DeRogatis, and Wee Willie Wilkin. Annoyed by my kicking tape, during a game Wee Willie Wilkin once said, "When Groza kicks, someone go in there and steal his tape."

The most physical games came against the San Francisco 49ers and the New York Yankees, our chief rivals in the AAFC. When we joined the NFL in 1950, Detroit and New York always illicited the most "spirited" play. I would characterize these games as hard-hitting, but not as dirty.

I don't believe that professional football in my day was any more violent or dirty than today's games. Yes, you'd have that occasional guy who would do some nasty tricks (usually in retribution for a cheap shot), like punching, biting, or spearing an opponent. But overall the game wasn't that dirty.

Chuck Bednarik, the Hall-of-Fame linebacker for the Eagles, rep-utably was the dirtiest football player in the game's history. At least that seems to be the impression many viewers receive when they hear Chuck speak or watch that replay of his infamous hit on Frank Gif-ford. He hit Gifford from the blind side, but it was a good, clean shot. Bednarik's solid hits later became confused by later generations of football fans with dirty play. But he was not a dirty football player.

There was some trash-talking among the opponents, but it wasn't predominant. Every once in a while I'd go up against some guy who would talk, and really not much happened as a result of these conver-sations. I can tell you, however, that when I played there was not as much finger-pointing and ridiculing of the members of the other team as you see today.

Today's media unfortunately like to focus their cameras and com-mentaries on the frequent displays of unsportmanship—taunting, dancing, and high stepping, etc.—which has eroded the aesthetic beauty of the game. These antics have deflected our attention from the strategy, speed, balance, athleticism, intensity, and contact which makes the game of football such a popular American pastime.

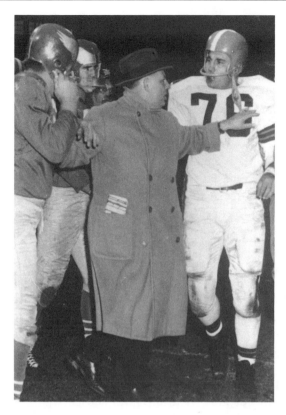

One of the few times that I lost my composure happened in a game against the Eagles in 1954. After our 6-0 victory I had to be separated from an opponent who (I thought) intentionally elbowed me in the face. *Fred Bottomer, Cleveland State University Archives*

* * *

Enough has already been said and written about the infamous Paul Brown/Art Modell conflict. I respect both men, and I don't see the point in delineating all of the issues that made it difficult for these two dynamic individuals to work together. They both seemed, however, to get things patched up near the end of Paul's life.

Simply stated, the reason that Paul and Art did not get along centered on Paul Brown's unwillingness to give up complete control of the football team. Since 1946 Paul had handpicked his players and coaches, had called the plays, and had handled contract talks. When Art Modell became the principal owner of the Browns in 1961, he did not want to stay in the background. He wished to be an aggressive, hands-on owner. Even though the Browns had posted winning records over the last several years, they had not been to the NFL championship game since 1957. Modell was anxious to bring a title back to Cleveland.

You can't blame either Art or Paul for the struggle for power which ended up with Paul's departure. Paul was accustomed to having full command of his squad, but Art had invested his own hard-earned money in the franchise and desperately felt a responsibility to take an active role in the running of the football team. Where Mickey McBride would rarely attend a practice session, Art Modell seemed to be always around. Art wanted to be a part of the team.

Art's sense of humor and friendliness attracted the interest of the players. Some players sensed that Art would listen to their complaints about Paul Brown, and they began to express their disenchantment directly to Art, who would share their concerns with the head coach.

The hostility between the two men diminished over the years. Art came over at the recent 1964 Championship Team 30th anniversary luncheon and Mary Brown, Paul's wife, was there. Art came over to talk to her to tell her how nice it was to see her there. Paul and Art would also meet at the owners' meetings when Paul ran the Bengals.

My relations with Art were and still remain cordial. I will always be indebted to Art for convincing Paul Brown to reactivate me in 1961 and for giving me the chance to kick another seven years for the Browns.

I do regret something I said to a reporter (off the record) when Paul was fired. I told this reporter that "the Browns will never be the same again without Paul." I didn't mean that the Browns were going to fall apart; I just was acknowledging the fact that a long and glorious era of Browns football was coming to a close. I had known Paul for over twenty years and had played ball for him for seventeen consecutive seasons. His firing had to affect me. Art did not interpret my remarks about Paul in the same way. I'm afraid that he took my comments very personally.

I regret the misunderstanding because I have great respect for Art and for what he is trying to accomplish with his team.

* * *

I had the good fortune to play alongside many football legends—the Hall-of-Famers. These gifted athletes were responsible for keeping the Browns dynasty intact.

Jim Brown: What he accomplished in only nine years (1957-1965) will never be duplicated. He averaged 5.2 yards a carry, led the NFL in rushing eight times, and never missed a game. Jim gained over 12,000 yards rushing during a period when we played twelve- and fourteen-game seasons. Teams play sixteen regular-season games now.

Jim was very strong at 6'2" and 232 pounds. He is the one that all backs are judged by. Jim possessed a very strong torso and shrugged off a lot of tacklers with his arms. And he had great maneuverability. He could instantly crack through an opening and expertly follow his interference. Jim masterfully set up blocks for his linemen; he'd make a move and then smartly cut off the block. He was an easy guy to block for. He was strong enough where it would usually require more than one man to bring him down. Added to this was a runner with sprinter's speed. He also caught the ball well. Although he didn't get to throw many passes, he could throw a football very long and accurately.

Jim Brown was the most confident football player in history. Those who didn't know Jim personally, however, would confuse his self-assurance with arrogance. Some of Jim's on-the-field habits may have led people to believe that he was cocky. For instance, after he was tackled Jim would very slowly rise up off the ground and walk back to the huddle. Many observers interpreted Jim's after-the-play lethargy as a smug effort to draw attention to himself.

In reality, Jim took his time in order to catch his breath, to reload the cannon, in a sense. The Browns designed their offense around Jim Brown; therefore he was asked to carry the ball much more frequently than had any other running back in history. He needed to preserve his strength and energy so that he could take advantage of an opening in the line which could lead to a long scamper.

Jim seemed egotistical to those who didn't know him. During interviews, for example, he delivered answers and observations with a seriousness (and a blunt honesty) that was misread as aloofness. He rarely smiled in front of the camera or on the football field. There is a simple explanation for Jim's apparent stoicism. Jim understood that he was a gifted athlete, and no one had higher expectations than did Jim himself. To reach peak performance, he engaged the powers of a very keen mind. He was the most focused player that I have ever known. When the subject was his vocation—football, he was all business. And he exerted a form of concentration and effort that made him achieve what no other football player had ever accomplished, before or since.

Jim Brown is back on the Browns payroll. He works as an intermediary between the players and the coaching staff. Jim also counsels young players and has been called upon to give motivational talks to the entire team.

At a recent luncheon Jim Brown stated that I never let them (the Browns) down. I am happy to have Jim's respect. He certainly has mine.

Jim Brown and John Wooten were and still are good friends. Jim also is a good friend of Dick Shafrath's. When I played for the Browns my closest buddies were Vince Costello, Galen Fiss, Otto Graham, Marion Motley, Paul Wiggin, Lou Rymkus, John Morrow, and Dante Lavelli. It's always great when we get together and talk over old times.

Len Ford: Ford came from the Los Angeles Dons when the AAFC folded in 1950. He had attended the University of Michigan. As an offensive tackle, I had to block this hard-charging defensive end in practice. And his steady aggressiveness, of course, made me a better blocker. I couldn't relax . Lenny was large; he stood 6'6" and weighed 250 pounds, quite big in those days. He was rushing the passer all of the time. Like Marion, he had big thighs. When you tried to block him, he'd give you his leg.

In a game against the Chicago Cardinals, Len was giving running back Pat Harder a tough time. Harder had trouble blocking him. And Lenny was antagonizing him with expressions like, "What's the matter, Pat?" On a subsequent play, Pat smashed him right in the face and broke Lenny's cheekbone. There were no reprisals. Len was out for a long time, but returned that season wearing one of those big, cage-like face protectors.

Frank Gatski: Frank was an original Brown; he was with the first Browns team in 1946. He attended Marshall College. He was a Rock of Gibraltar in the middle of the line, a big, strong guy. He worked as a coal miner in West Virginia which developed him physically. Frank also was one of the first professional football players to incorporate weight training into his workout regimen.

When the Browns formed in 1946, we all played offense and defense. It boiled down eventually (1948) that players began to play on only one side of the ball (offense or defense). Gatski played center and was very consistent at snapping the ball. Never getting rattled, Frank snapped for field goals, extra points, and punts. Very quiet, you wouldn't even know if Frank were around.

Otto Graham: Otto was the greatest quarterback in NFL history. During his entire career, from 1946-1955, Otto guided the Browns to ten consecutive championship games, winning seven. How many times a team gets into the championship game and how many times that team wins that game reflects the quality of the quarterback. He was our leader.

Standing 6 feet and weighing 190 pounds, Otto was a fine all-around athlete. In high school and at Northwestern he not only was an All-American tailback, but he was a sensational basketball player. Otto even played pro basketball one year at Rochester.

Like me, Otto signed a contract to play for Paul Brown while he still was in the service. (Otto was in the Navy.) Otto was the first player that Paul signed, and I was the second.

I was in the service when Otto played at Northwestern, and the first time I met him was in the first Browns training camp of 1946. Cliff Lewis, from Duke University, was the original starter, but

A rare photograph of Otto holding the ball for me (Otto wasn't my regular holder) in a game against the New York Yankees in 1947.
John Nash, Cleveland State University Archives

soon Otto became number one. He was a splendid runner and pinpoint passer. And Otto was physically and mentally tough.

Otto tells that story that when you played for him, Paul Brown would make you angry, but when you got out of football and you began coaching you wanted to be just like him

After Otto retired following the 1955 season when we once again won the NFL title, the team couldn't find a suitable replacement until Frank Ryan appeared in the next decade.

Leroy Kelly: Jim Brown's replacement at fullback (1964-1972), Leroy was similar to Bobby Mitchell in that he had those same darting moves. By anticipating the snap count, Leroy could hit the hole quicker than any back that I saw. Leroy was also the top punt returner in the NFL for a number of years.

Dante Lavelli: An original Brown, from Ohio State, our gifted offensive end, we called him "Glue Fingers." Dante's teammate at the other end was Mac Speedie, giving us as fine a pair of ends as you would ever hope to find. Dante caught the ball well in a crowd and was absolutely fearless when going over the middle to catch a pass. Dante had great moves and seemed always to have beaten his defender. He had soft hands. We remain very close friends and see each other often.

When Otto would be scrambling to avoid tacklers you would always hear Lavelli (in a loud shrill) screaming, "Otto, Otto, Otto!" Dante thought that he could catch the ball every time, and he usually did.

Mike McCormack: Mike came to us from the Baltimore Colts. Our right tackle from 1954 to 1962, Mike always played consistent, outstanding football. He also played some linebacker. Mike is now the president of the Carolina Panthers.

Bobby Mitchell: He was a scatback for us from 1958-1961. Bobby maneuvered smoothly and possessed lightning speed. He suddenly could react to situations. That was the greatest backfield of all time—Brown and Mitchell. When he made a cut he didn't slow down. Bobby today is an executive with the Washington Redskins.

Marion Motley: That first training camp in Bowling Green (1946) when we were all trying to make the football team we had a scrimmage in nearby Toledo. In those days we played both offense and defense. Rosters were limited to only 33 men, so you had a better chance of making the team if you could play on both sides of the ball. I felt at a disadvantage as compared with the vastly more experienced competitors at camp because I had only played three games of college freshman football.

Well, in this particular scrimmage, hoping to impress the coaching staff with my defensive prowess, I decided to tackle Marion Motley, all 240 pounds of him, head on. I saw stars. From that point on I never tried to tackle him head on; I tried to get him from the side and pull him down because he had enormously powerful thighs. Marion was already 27 with a wife and four children when he arrived in camp. His Herculean frame had been built up by his recent employment in a steel mill. He was a man; most of us were still boys.

Motley played at McKinley High School in the birthplace of football, Canton, Ohio. Paul knew about Marion when he coached at Massillon. Canton McKinley was (and still is and always will be) Massillon's greatest rival. Marion had gone out to Nevada with Jimmy Akin, who was the coach there. Jimmy Akin and Paul Brown were friends, and I'm sure that Paul was in touch with Jimmy to find out how Marion performed. Marion was also at Great Lakes when Paul was head coach. And Paul knew what Marion could do, not only in high school but later.

One of the humorous sights I remember about Marion was when we had the opposing team backed up and we sent Marion in on defense. He played linebacker in goal-line or short-yardage situations. "Loosen up, Marion. Loosen up," the coach would shout. Marion then would start very animatedly to shrug his shoulders.

We used to play more exhibition games then, including a contest at the Akron Rubber Bowl. During the exhibition season we'd also fly to the West Coast and play both LA and San Francisco. (My first plane ride, in fact, didn't happen until I was a Brown. I was scared to death.) We'd stay at Randolph Hearst's ranch. I recall one time when Marion Motley tried to ride this uncooperative horse. He slapped the horse on the back and the animal took off, and Marion couldn't stop it. All of us laughed hysterically.

Motley was dangerous as a receiver, too. One time, Otto Graham was about ready to be swarmed under by a charging defensive end when he decided to drop a short pass off in the backfield to Marion—the screen pass was born.

He was an outstanding blocker. In those days we were running into five-man and six-man lines, and Marion was always relegated to blocking an end or mopping up as an extra back in pass blocking.

We didn't wear masks in those days and I can remember one game where Marion kept being punched by this defenseman in the face. He even put his hand in Marion's mouth. Weary of being accosted, Marion bit the guy's hand.

Marion had a partial in his front teeth, and during a game it came out when he was carrying the ball. He said, "Time out." The official and everybody started looking for his false tooth. He found it in a cleat hole. He put it in his mouth and said, "Okay, let's go."

The Browns were the first football team to have blacks on the roster. I can remember that in some towns our black players couldn't stay in the same lodgings with us. They could only be housed in hotels that catered to "Negroes Only." All of this seems hard to believe now.

Marion was required to do a lot of things, like blocking and carrying the ball. He had a marvelous demeanor about him. He was a real competitor. One of the most outstanding runs that Marion made was against Pittsburgh. He got hit, and his helmet flew off, and he kept running over 50 yards for the touchdown up the sideline. I wouldn't want a steady diet of him if I were on defense.

Marion became the leading rusher in AAFC history, and he averaged a remarkable 5.7 yards per carry.

Today Marion spends much of his time on the golf course.

Chuck Noll: Got in as a coach, rather than as a player, where he played at the guard position (1953-1959). As a player he was a student of the game, and Chuck later became a masterful coach of the Pittsburgh Steelers, winning four Super Bowls.

Paul Warfield: Paul arrived as a rookie from Ohio State in 1964. Paul had great moves and was the smoothest and most graceful receiver I have ever seen. And after he caught the football he became a dangerous running back, as he outmaneuvered the defensemen with tremendous ease. He made razor sharp cuts and ran precision pass patterns, making him an easy target the quarterback. Paul possessed extraordinary leaping ability and was not afraid to catch the ball in the crowd or to run across the middle. He had such great speed that he opened a little air between himself and the defensive backs so that he could protect himself from getting clobbered.

Bill Willis: Bill Willis, one of many Buckeyes who played for the Browns, was a middle guard, the guy who lined up over the center in a five-man line. Bill played between 1946-1953. I remember

Mike Scarry, an excellent center who had played for the Rams, was pitted against Willis during the 1946 tryout. Paul Brown wanted to see how well Bill Willis could handle this veteran blocker. Right then and there Bill Willis demonstrated his famous quickness. Willis would hit Mike so quickly that Scarry kept stepping on the quarterback's foot as he was rocked backwards by Willis. Scarry had an awful time getting into his blocking position. He never went up against a player in the years that he played with the Rams who could do that to him. After this impressive debut, the Browns signed Bill.

Willis was fast; he had run track in school. Bill had a lot of roaming ability. He could make a lot of tackles away from the center of the line. He was strong. He'd curl up like a spring; he had a very explosive start at the line of scrimmage. He'd hit the center right under his shoulder pads. He'd push back the center and stand him up. And then he would find where the ball was and go after it.

Bill has a magnificent voice, deep and resonant. He is a marvelous public speaker.

Most of the Hall of Famers were on great teams and played a long time. Your chances are enhanced when you play on championship teams. It's no surprise that the Packers, Steelers, Bears, Cowboys, and Browns have lot of Hall of Famers.

* * *

In addition to the Hall-of-Famers I had the privilege to play alongside hundreds of excellent football players in my 21 seasons as a Brown. They reflected an enormous range of talent and personalities.

Tony Adamle: Tony and I were freshman teammates at Ohio State. A tough, hard-nosed linebacker (1947-1951, 1954), Tony was our captain and leader on defense. He also was our third fullback. He became a doctor.

Chet Adams: Chet attended Ohio University and played with the Cleveland Rams before the war. Paul signed him in our first year (1946), and he played tackle for us through 1948.

Maurice Bassett: Bassett replaced our great fullback Marion Motley, who retired after the 1953 season.   From Langston, Oklahoma, Maurice helped us to reclaim NFL titles in 1954 and 1955.

Erich Barnes: A fun-loving guy, Erich played with the Giants before he came to us in 1965 as a defensive back.

Johnny Brewer: Our big tight end in the early 1960's, Johnny attended the University of Mississippi. I scouted him the year I had hurt my back (1960) and couldn't play.   His teammates nicknamed him "stone hands" because he had trouble catching the ball, but Brewer was a superb blocker. He also showed enough flexibility and natural ability to convert to the linebacker position in 1966

Rex Bumgardner: Rex made two huge plays in the 1950 championship game against Los Angeles. The diving catch he made in the end zone near the end of the contest put us back in the game. And another great catch set up my winning kick.

Hopalong Cassady: The Browns picked him up from Detroit for the 1962 season, Paul Brown's last as head coach. Cassady won the Heisman trophy at Ohio State in 1955 and had a good career at Detroit.

Monte Clark: Monte attended the University of Southern California. The Browns·acquired Monte from the San Francisco 49ers in 1963, and he performed brilliantly at offensive tackle through 1969. Monte remained in the coaching business after his playing days were over. He's coached with Shula, and later was an assistant coach with Bill Walsh on those splendid 49er teams.   Now he's back with Shula and the Dolphins.

Gary Collins: The Browns selected Gary in the first round of the 1962 draft. Gary was a consensus All-American end at Maryland. A money player, Gary Collins caught the ball well in a crowd. Collins ran the post pattern between the goalposts beautifully. In the days when the goalposts stood on the goal line, clever receivers like Collins would use the posts as additional blockers to shield themselves from opposing players. Gary sometimes swung around the goalposts in order to get open for a pass. When he came back in 1994 for for the reunion of our 1964 NFL championship team, he recreated one of those three famous receptions and the fans loved it.

Don Colo: Don played defensive tackle and captain from 1953-1958. We got him from the Baltimore Colts. Along with Bob Gain, Don really anchored the middle of the line. Don owns a trucking company in Arizona.

Vince Costello: I've always told Vince that even as I got older I could still beat him in a foot race. He was a rugged and enthusiastic linebacker (1957-1966). Like Alex Agase who played linebacker for us in the late 1940's and early 1950's, Vince expertly read offensive formations. Vince anticipated what offensive play was being called, and this talent enabled him to make many big plays for us.

Vince is a restaurant owner in Kansas City. We visit each other frequently.

Ernie Davis: Ernie was a terrific kid. I regret that I never had a chance to play with Ernie because leukemia took Ernie away from us before he could even take a single hand off. The Browns traded Bobby Mitchell to the Washington Redskins in order to have the chance to draft (he was the first collegiate drafted in 1962) this gifted, All-American running back from Syracuse. As an Orangeman, Ernie broke most of Jim Brown's records and was projected to be a Hall-of-Fame caliber back in the pros. Many believed that the Browns would have started the greatest backfield in NFL history had Ernie survived. He was that good.

Ernie knew that he was dying, but he kept fighting his illness and kept hoping for a cure. The players and coaches also understood his condition. But the media, displaying noteworthy sensitivity for Ernie and his family, refused to divulge the ominous details concerning Ernie's health. Nonetheless, the public sensed that something was terribly wrong. When Art Modell asked Ernie in a pre-season game (in August of 1962) to walk to midfield under the glare of spotlights to be introduced, close to 80,000 fans exploded in a thunderous standing ovation.

Art Modell was deeply affected by Ernie's death, he had become very attached to this gentle and brave young man. (Art has always kept a photograph of Ernie on his office desk.) Art has said that the saddest day of his life came in May of 1963 when Ernie finally succumbed to leukemia.

Most of the Browns traveled to Ernie's funeral in Elmira, New York. In the procession to the cemetery I remember being touched by the grief. Both men and women, black and white, wept openly. Elmira loved Ernie. We all did.

What might have been—the dream backfield of Jim Brown and Ernie Davis. *Cleveland State University Archives*

Galen Fiss: Replaced an injured Chuck Noll at linebacker in 1957 and became a brilliant starting linebacker through 1966. He was our captain and leader and one of the defensive heroes in our championship victory over the Colts in 1964.

Don Fleming: Our talented starting safety and a real pleasant guy, Don was from Shadyside (near Martins Ferry) and later attended the University of Florida. After only three years, Don was quickly becoming one of the finest defensive backs in the NFL. But Don tragically was electrocuted in the off-season in June of 1963. The Browns retired his #46.

Bobby Franklin: Bobby was a fine defensive back and my holder for a few years. Bobby enjoyed teasing fellow Mississippian Johnny Brewer and possessed a very thick Southern accent. One time Bobby wanted me to fly down to his home state to give a speech in a town I thought was "Jupiter," but I finally figured out that Bobby was really saying "Tupelo."   Today, Bobby is a coach.

Bob Gain: Gain was a University of Kentucky All-American and the Outland Trophy winner as the nation's top collegiate linemen. He was a Pro Bowl-caliber defensive tackle and also did some placekicking (1952, 1954-1964). He lives in the Cleveland area, and we see him at Browns games.

Abe Gibron: Abe was big and fast. He wanted to run every play behind him because he had such a quick charge. Abe played left guard and I played left tackle (1950-1956). I had to really get off the ball because if I didn't, I looked like I was standing still. We had a contest of sorts to see who would get off the ball faster and first into the guy we were blocking. He was a member of a group of Browns players who proclaimed themselves as the Filthy Five because they never allowed their practice uniforms to be washed.

Horace Gillom: An outstanding end and punter who played during our golden years (1947-1956), Horace had played for Paul at Massillon. He made many big plays for us. Horace was a clutch performer.

Bill Glass: We got Bill from Detroit in 1962 where he had been the Lions No. 1 draft pick in 1957. Bill was big and perhaps the fastest defensive end in football at the time. Glass anchored the line with Paul Wiggin on the other side. They were as good a pair of ends as you'd find.

Bill Glass was very religious, but certainly not on the field. He would charge at a quarterback with satanic fury. Today Bill Glass is a prison minister. He also speaks at church revivals, sharing the stage with evangelists like Billy Graham.

Ernie Green: Green Bay actually selected Green in the 1962 draft, but Vince Lombardi offered Ernie to the Browns after Ernie Davis became sick with leukemia.

If he weren't backing up Jim Brown, Ernie would have been recognized a lot more. He was an excellent back, a terrific blocker, and a fine receiver. But his role was to block for Jim Brown, which he did without complaint. Jim and Ernie made a formidable pair in our backfield.

Handsome, urbane and articulate, Ernie looks like he just stepped out of the cover of some gentleman's magazine. He is a business-man in Dayton.

Gene Hickerson: Gene was a superb guard for 14 seasons (1958-1960, 1962-1972) and deserves to be in the Hall of Fame. As good a guard as we ever had. Just ask anyone who ran behind his blocks. He was an outstanding pulling guard, and carved out countless holes for Jimmy Brown. I have no idea why he isn't in the Hall of Fame.

Gene is another Brown who remained in Cleveland after his retire-ment. He is a very successful restaurateur.

Les Horvath: A former Heisman Trophy winner (1944) from Ohio State, Les played one year (1949) for the Browns. He didn't play much for us and later became a dentist.

Jim Houston: Another Buckeye (and Massillon Tiger) and our de-fensive captain and linebacker (1960-1972), Jim could also play defensive end. Jim was big and extremely quick.

Lin Houston: Jim's older brother, Lin played guard for the Browns from 1946-1953. He was on the great Massillon teams which Paul Brown coached. He became an All-American at Ohio State. Lin was the strong, silent type. His actions on the field spoke much louder than his words.

Tommy James: A steady defensive back, Tommy also played at Massillon before going on to Ohio State to play under Paul Brown. After a couple of years in Detroit, Tommy joined us in 1948. Tom-my followed Don Greenwood as my holder. He was an outstand-ing holder for me.

Walter Johnson: Walt was an outstanding All-Pro defensive tackle (1965-1972). I recall on the plane ride back from a playoff loss to Minnesota when he started screaming from frostbite. (The field was frozen during the game, and Walt kept putting his hand down on the frozen turf. He had worn gloves but that wasn't enough.) We were on the bus going toward the airport and all the medical equipment was on a truck en route to the airport. All of a sudden we all hear these blood curdling screams. His fingers were frozen and were thawing out. We thought all the way home on the plane that he would lose some fingers.

Dub Jones: Teammate Warren Lahr nicknamed Dub "Six O'Clock" because he was a bean pole, tall and thin, straight up and down. Dub played for us between 1948-1955. Caught six touchdown passes in one game—a record. A graduate of Tulane, Dub was acquired from the AAFC Miami Seahawks. Dub was a good target because of his speed, height, and concentration. He turned the corners well. Later Dub became a valuable receiver's coach for Blanton Collier. Dub is in the lumber business in Louisiana.

Jim Kanicki: This big defensive tackle from Michigan State had his finest performance against the Colts in the 1964 championship. He is a businessman in Ashtabula, Ohio. Jim was always one of my favorites.

John Kissell: Came from Buffalo with Ratterman, Gibron, and Bumgardner in 1950 when we joined the NFL. He was a tough competitor for six years. I remember when John once made the crack (in reference to our salaries) to the guys in the locker room, "Turn the lights off; it's costing too much money."

Edgar Jones: Edgar was nicknamed Special Delivery. The stocky Edgar Jones was especially lethal on the quick hitters (1946-1949).

Warren Lahr: Warren attended Western Reserve University, and he was a very smart football player. He also possessed great athletic skills. Warren played tennis very well. In excellent condition (even in the off-season) Warren was a skillful defensive back for 12 seasons, 1948-1959. He died at a young age.

Walt Michaels: Walt played linebacker for us from 1952-1961. He was a bright guy, who later became head coach of the Jets.

Dick Modzelewski: Dick was nicknamed "Little Mo" despite being taller than his brother Ed who was called "Big Mo." Dick came to us from the Giants and was a key factor in our winning the title in 1964. Dick played smart and physical football at his defensive tackle position. He later became an assistant coach for us.

Ed Modzelewski: While Dick was a broad and husky lineman, brother Ed was a hard-driving and quick fullback. He slowed down, however, after he broke his leg, and he retired earlier than he had anticipated.

John Morrow: John was one of my roommates. Dedicated and serious, John lifted weights before weight lifting was popular. He, in fact, brought his weight set to our room. At training camp in 1960, the year I hurt my back and had to quit (and John's first year with the Browns), John placed a massive trunk on the bed that I usually slept on. He then pushed his own bed right under the window. I thought that John was attempting to exert his authority, that he was trying to take over. But that wasn't the case at all. After this unusual introduction, we became and remain good friends.

John was a Pro Bowl center twice in his seven years as a Brown.

Jim Ninowski: A Brown from 1958-1959 and 1962-1966, Jim probably threw the ball as long and as hard as any quarterback in football. His ball possessed a tight spiral. Jim was also my holder, and when he would place his very large hands on the ball, I sometimes lost my concentration from the target spot on the ball because it took Jim so long for him to move his massive hands away from the ball as he set it in position He became a successful Detroit businessman.

Darrell Palmer: A two-way tackle, in 1950, in our first NFL game against the Philadelphia Eagles, I hurt my shoulder and Darrell ended up playing offensive left tackle.

Darrell roomed with the colorful, tobacco-chewing Chubby Grigg. Darrell once asked for a sip of Chubby's pop, not knowing that Chubby had moments before spit tobacco into the can. He took a sip of it, and everyone but Darrell had a great laugh.

I can still hear Darrell saying "Dad Gummit' when he was upset.

Bernie Parrish: Bernie attended the University of Florida and played defensive back for the Browns from 1959-1966. Bernie was bright, possessed great quickness, and was a vicious tackler. Always drawing up defenses, talking to the coaches, having team meetings, Bernie seemed almost hyperactive.

Ara Parseghian: Ara ran well at running back for us (1948-1949) until he pulled his hip out of its socket. After that he walked with a limp. He went on to enormous success as head coach of the Fighting Irish.

Don Paul: Don was a smart defensive back (1954-1958). One time the other team had punted, and everyone was hovering around the ball waiting for the ball to stop rolling when Don came crashing in, picked up the ball, and dashed right between everyone for a touchdown.

Floyd Peters: A tough defensive tackle for four years, 1959-1962, Floyd has become a very respected NFL coach. He still looks like a marine drill sergeant.

Milt Plum: He quarterbacked the Browns from 1957-1961. Drafted out of Penn State, the Browns thought that they had finally found Otto's successor. Milt possessed much natural ability, and he was good enough to withstand the challenge from a rookie signal-caller by the name of Len Dawson, who would later become a Hall-of-Fame quarterback with the Kansas City Chiefs.

He was critical of the fact that Paul Brown called the plays, and his outspokenness led to his being traded to Detroit.

George Ratterman: George was, on the surface, a "good, Catholic boy from Notre Dame." His brother, in fact, was a priest.

But there was a devilish side to this quarterback (1952-1956). In Washington before a game with the Redskins some of us decided to leave the hotel and walk to a movie theater. On the way we crossed a small bridge with arches running across the top. George suddenly climbed onto one of those spans and casually walked atop the arch while the rest of us chose to take the more traditional route.

While George was a student at Notre Dame, cars and taxis blocked his path as he attempted to cross an intersection. One car, in particular, jutted beyond the pedestrian lines. So George opened the guy's back door and walked through the car, opened the car door on the other side and continued walking.

George was always the last guy to leave the locker room, well, almost always. One time George knowingly locked equipment manager Morrie Kono in the locker room after a practice at League Park. Everyone was gone and Morrie couldn't get out. Poor Morrie spent the entire night in the locker room.

Seeking revenge, at the next practice, Morrie locked all of George's clothes in a trunk. George was unruffled when he noticed his empty cubicle. George nonchalantly proceeded to exit the locker area wearing his sweatsuit. "See you tomorrow, Morrie," George said, as he strolled by Kono.

Ratterman also became famous for being the first quarterback to wear a radio in his helmet. The device made its debut in 1957 in an exhibition game against the Lions at the Akron Rubber Bowl. As the skies darkened George became nervous because he thought that he would be a walking lighting rod. The Lions also thought that they could destroy the communication between Paul Brown and his quarterback by kicking George's helmet.   But the real reason that the experiment ended was when Ratterman was hearing other things in his receiver besides the coach's instructions. George heard, at one point, a voice giving directions about the upcoming halftime show.

Ray Renfro: Although he played in three Pro-Bowl games, Ray didn't get the recognition he deserved. Extremely fast, he ran a 9.5 for the 100-yard dash at North Texas State. He made a lot of big catches for us (1952-1963).

Ray was very popular with both teammates and fans   I can still hear Ray's signature greeting, "How you doin' podner?"

Walter Roberts: He was called The Flea because of his diminutive size. Despite being the smallest player in the NFL at the time, Walt compensated with tremendous, slashing speed and returned many kicks for long gainers from 1964-1966.

Frank Ryan: Our quarterback from 1962-1968 and the last Browns QB to win an NFL championship. Frank threw a very accurate and soft pass. Extremely intelligent, Frank earned a PhD. After a stint as athletic director at Yale, he now is at Rice.

Lou Rymkus: Lou called himself "The Heel" after I acquired my nickname. He came to the Browns via Notre Dame and the Washington Redskins. Lou played offensive tackle from 1946-1951. He played well enough to get Hall-of-Fame consideration.

He used to kid Paul Brown: "No wonder we go through all these fundamental drills, there are so many Ohio State guys on our team."

Lou once declared, "I once broke my leg and set it myself and stayed right in the game." His nickname was "The Battler."

Lou Saban: Lou Saban, one of our captains, was an intense linebacker (1946-1949). He later went on to coach the Buffalo Bills.

John Sandusky: John, after his playing days, became a faithful, long-time assistant coach with Don Shula at Baltimore and Miami. He took over the right tackle spot when Lou Rymkus retired in 1951. We still keep in close touch.

Dick Shafrath: Dick replaced me at left tackle in 1960. A consistent Pro-Bowler, he possessed great speed and intensity. He was the best downfield blocker that I ever saw. This former Ohio State Buckeye later became a state senator.

Jim Shofner: Jim played cornerback with us from 1958-1963. Jim was very smart and later went into coaching. He is now with Buffalo.

Don Shula: Don is in the Hall of Fame as a coach, but he was a solid cornerback for the Browns for a couple of seasons, 1951-1952. He later coached under future Browns head coach Blanton Collier at Kentucky. Don, in fact, contacted Blanton when Paul Brown was fired to ask Blanton to join him in Baltimore. But Blanton got the head coaching job here.

Don is still the head coach of the Miami Dolphins and is one of the most respected men in pro football.

Jim Ray Smith: A big, quick, and agile guard (1956-1962), Jim Ray Smith was an outstanding pulling guard, one of the fastest to have ever played that position. He made the Pro Bowl a number of times.

Mac Speedie: Mac was an extraordinary receiver for us (1946-1952). He jumped the Browns to go to Canada. If he hadn't played Canadian football, Mac would be in the Hall of Fame. He was that good.

Overcoming Perthes as a child, Mac was deceptively fast, had soft hands, and possessed great jumping ability. He had been a fine a college hurdler. Mac teamed up with Dante Lavelli to give the Browns the best tandem of ends in that era.

Paul Wiggin: Paul was a student of the game. I used to have to block Paul in practice all of the time. And it was tough because this defensive end (1957-1967) never let up. He worked hard all of the time, reflective of his personality.

Paul is in the personnel department of the Minnesota Vikings.

John Wooten: John played nine years (1959-1967) with us. He was part of the best guard tandem in football—Hickerson and Wooten. He could run block and pass block as well as any guard. John Wooten and Jim Brown are close friends.

John works with the Philadelphia Eagles.

* * *

In 1960 I hurt my back in a scrimmage at training camp, and I was out of football that year and thought I was out of football for good. As I retreated into the backfield with an opponent who was trying to get around my block, I didn't realize that a back had missed a block behind me. Well, the guy that I was blocking charged into me, and I subsequently tripped over someone on the ground behind me. My cleats dug into the ground, and I fell over backwards onto my back. The pain made it difficult even to walk, and I really thought I was going to need surgery. But eventually the pain diminished after about half the season.

The Browns kept me employed, however, as a college scout rather than as a football player. I'd leave Cleveland on Friday and arrive at the desired college campus that afternoon. On Saturday I'd watch the game from the press box and write down my evaluations of a particular player the Browns were interested in drafting. For example, I scouted Bobby Crespino and Johnny Brewer, two future Browns, when they played at the University of Mississippi.

I recall a Preston "High Pockets" Powell of Grambling. The Grambling team was going through a formal practice, and Preston, who had already graduated, stood on the sidelines in street clothes. Soon Preston and some friends began throwing a football around, and later Preston ran some pass patterns. I was impressed with the precision of his patterns, his speed, and his soft hands. In fact, I believed that Powell was a better prospect than anyone on the field. So I recommended that the Browns sign him not only for his athletic potential, but because he had already graduated. The Browns took my advice and signed him.

Another scouting assignment took me to rural Mississippi. I was driving a car in the early morning hours from Memphis when, on a quiet, country road, I got stopped by a fully robed group of Ku Klux Klansmen. "Oh, no!" I thought, as they forced me to pull off to the side of the road. (My childhood recollection of cross burnings near Martins Ferry ignited my concern.)

They were very suspicious about my presence and firmly inquired about my reason for being in the vicinity. Trying to suppress my nervousness, I answered, "I'm a scout with the Cleveland Browns; I'm looking for football players."

"We'd like to see some identification," one of them asked.

I presented my driver's license, and I don't know if they recognized my name, but they let me go, thank goodness.

One other scouting adventure didn't conclude so peacefully. I traveled to Bowling Green to scout a game between Cal Poly and BGSU. Before the game, I talked to some of the football players (on both squads) in whom the Browns had shown some interest. After the game, the Cal Poly team boarded a bus going to the nearby Toledo Airport.

That early evening, as I drove home on the Ohio Turnpike, a fog creeped in and thickened to the degree that I was forced to follow the middle line of the turnpike to keep going. I was very anxious to get home to my family. As I pulled into my driveway, I heard on the car radio that the Cal Poly plane had crashed near Toledo because of the fog. Some of the boys that I met earlier in the day had been killed. It took me a long time to get over this tragedy.

In 1961, the NFL expanded roster sizes because of the emergence of another league in 1960, the American Football League (AFL).

The NFL wanted to keep football players so they wouldn't be available for the other league. So they expanded the size of the squads in order to carry specialists. And with that I was invited to come back. I was working with the kickers. And the Browns decided to activate me.

When Art bought the club I became acquainted with him. My office was in the Terminal Tower. He said he was having dinner at the Kon-Tiki in the Hotel Cleveland. I went over and introduced myself to him.

He asked me, "Can you still kick?"

I said, "Yes."

So he came out to Berea High School Field and held some footballs for me. I impressed Art so much that he persuaded Paul to reactivate me as a kicker.

On October 7, 1962, the Browns treated me to Lou Groza Day at Municipal Stadium. My wife, children, mother, brothers Frank and Alex, along with some dignitaries from Martins Ferry stood on the field near me as I spoke to the crowd. I contributed to our win over the Cowboys (19-10) after the ceremony.

Being honored at halftime in Cleveland Stadium on October 7, 1962. My youngest son, Judd, found the football more interesting than his dad's speech. *Henry M. Barr*

About two years after this tribute the Browns finally returned to the championship game for the first time since 1957. Blanton Collier was in his second year as head coach, and we were coming off of an impressive 10-4 record in 1963. Jim Brown was at his peak as a running back. The previous season he rushed for 1,863 yards, the most ever by a running back (up to that point) in NFL history. During the 1963 season Jim averaged an unbelievable 6.4 yards per carry, establishing another record.

After many years of searching for a quarterback to replace Otto Graham, the Browns finally found an intelligent signal-caller from Rice University—Frank Ryan. A rookie by the name of Paul Warfield added speed and superb pass-catching skills to the receiving corps. There was no more potent offense in professional football. However, the Browns defense surrendered a good deal of real estate during the regular season which contributed to the reason why the odds makers gave the overwhelming edge to the better balanced Baltimore Colts.

The powerful Colts were led by future Hall-of-Famers Johnny Unitas, Raymond Berry, Gino Marchetti, and Jim Parker. Their coach was a brilliant, young Paul Brown disciple—Don Shula. Most observers agreed that playing in front of the home town fans would be the only edge that the Browns could claim. But we players knew of another edge—the game-planning genius of Blanton Collier.

After a scoreless first half, I kicked one of the most important field goals in my life, a 43-yarder, to put us on the board and, more significantly, to give us some much-needed momentum. Gary Collins snared three long passes for touchdowns from Ryan, and our underrated defense, led by the relentless pursuit of linebacker Galen Fiss and tackle Jim Kanicky, stalked and disrupted Unitas, who was only able to pass for 95 yards. 80,000 fans went crazy at the game's end, as we accomplished the unthinkable, shutting out the Colts, 27-0.

The following year we met Lombardi's Packers in Green Bay and lost to them in the NFL championship game, 23-12. I felt that our 1965 team should have defeated the Packers. We had an 11-3 record coming into Lambeau Field, but the field conditions stifled our explosive offense and prevented us from playing up to our expectations.

Green Bay also had one heck of a team. This victory would catapult the Packers to the pedestal of professional football dominance for the next few years. This victory marked the emergence of the Green Bay dynasty.

Blanton Collier huddles with reporters following our stunning victory over the Colts. *Bernie Noble, Cleveland State University Archives*

* * *

In my next-to-last year (1966) against the New York Giants something quite humbling happened. I kicked off and ran downfield as this youthful Giant tried to block me. I dodged his pursuit and just as I turned to reach for the returner, he caught me with a block from the blind side. My feet went out from under me. His block lifted me, and I fell smack down on my back. While helping me up he said, "Excuse me, *Mr.* Groza."

I told him, "Great block."

I was thinking to myself—maybe it was time to retire.

The saddest day of my football life took place when I had to hang up the spikes. In 1968 I entered my twenty-second training camp believing that I could still kick in the NFL. I would not have tried to compete if I had thought differently.

The Browns, however, had Don Cockcroft, a talented placekicker from Adams State, and they figured it was better to go with the younger guy. Blanton Collier invited me to stay on and work with the kickers, but I declined.

I could have signed with the San Francisco 49ers. They asked me to fly out, but I didn't want to pick up and move my family and my insurance business to the West Coast. Cleveland was our home. Being released was a letdown because I still thought I could do it. But I concluded that the Browns wanted to get some younger guy in there. I was 44, and I had enjoyed a great career in Cleveland. I realized that I had nothing to prove by going somewhere else. I didn't have anything to gain at that point.

Right after retirement Jackie and I started attending the games as spectators. We still go to every home game and sit in those same seats. Football is still a very important part of our lives.

After retirement I continued with my insurance business. I was preparing all along for the day inevitable. If I had become a coach, I probably could not have survived all the coaching changes. The lifespan of a coach is short. I wasn't the kind of guy who liked going all over the country. I got the idea that I didn't want to be a coach in high school, where I had three different football coaches. My fourth child, Judd, was born in 1963, and I didn't want to travel all over the country. I had made a lot of contacts in my business. I was established.

At that time our kids were starting to play in high school, so we we went from pro football to watching high school ball. This made the transition easier. Everyday that I played I was getting ready for my retirement. That's the way it was. It was a good transition. Most of the guys that I played with made the transition into the working world (or the real world, as some would call it) very well. Dante Lavelli started a furniture business; Otto went into coaching; and Jim went to Hollywood.

In those days the salaries were not that large, so you had to have another source of income. Today, you don't have to do anything but play ball. Players can retire more easily. My generation of football players had to plan ahead. Those athletes today whose careers are cut short, who have to retire early, experience more problems than did my group. Many players make the mistake of not graduating from college.

A football player actually has some disadvantages after retirement because he has to prove his worth in the business world. In my case, I suspected that some people thought, "Sure, he can kick a football, but what else does he know?"

PART III

FOLLOW-THROUGH
Life After Football

"All of life is mastering the fundamentals, its stance, approach, contact and follow-through. Truth is where the toe meets the ball."

Lou Groza

* * *

My greatest thrill in football occurred after retirement when I was inducted into the Pro Football Hall of Fame in 1974. Dick McCann, the director of the Hall of Fame in Canton, called me at home and announced the news.

My family drove down to Ashland University as the announcement circulated through the local and national media. Three of our children—Jeff, Jill, and Jon—were students at Ashland at the time. Seemingly half of Berea and Ashland attended the Hall-of-Fame ceremonies. We were so happy to share the day with our family and friends.

The festivities began with a reception on Thursday where the 1974 Class assembled for the first time. The 1974 inductees included Tony Canadeo, Bill George, Night Train Lane, and me. Tony Canadeo played halfback for the Packers during the 1940's and became the first Packer to rush for over 1,000 yards. Bill George, the first of the great middle linebackers, made All-Pro 8 times for the Chicago Bears. Dick "Night Train" Lane, defensive back for the Rams, Cardinals, and Lions, once intercepted 14 passes in a season, a NFL record.

The reception was held at the Canton Hilton and was a closed affair for past inductees, the media and assorted NFL officials. On Friday morning we were introduced at the mayor's breakfast. We were seated at a high table, a dais. About 3,000 attended the 7:30 breakfast.

At lunch, the wives enjoyed a luncheon/fashion show. While the wives attended the show, the Hall of Famers and inductees went to Brookside Country Club for a luncheon. Each inductee stood up at this Friday luncheon and said a few words about what this induction meant to him. Past inductees also spoke, which added a fraternal atmosphere to the occasion.

On Friday evening we attended a formal dinner, a dinner which was sold out a year in advance. The four inductees were introduced and then escorted by some young ladies, members of the Queen's Court, who led us from the far end of a huge convocation center. When it was my turn to be introduced, the band played the "Ohio State Fight Song." What a thrill.

Then we moved to the middle of the arena, where we stood on a huge platform. And while we stood on the platform, a giant television screen showed highlights and clips of our performances on the gridiron. The presenters made a few remarks that night. (My presenter, Paul Brown, kept referring to me as "Louie" in his comments.) Then all of us returned to the hotel to prepare our speeches for the induction ceremony on Saturday.

On that hot July Saturday we rode in convertibles through Canton for the annual parade to the Hall of Fame. Spectators would actually arrive at the parade route at four o'clock in the morning for a good seat. Bleachers and a reviewing stand were set up alongside the road.

Swarms of fans waved and clapped, and I remember not having much strength in my arms (after the two-hour ride) as I repeatedly waved to the thousands of people who had been such enthusiastic and loyal supporters of me for so many years. Even the Martins Ferry High School Marching Band marched in the parade.

After the parade we had brunch at a private gathering for the 1974 inductees. Vice President Gerald Ford was the special guest speaker that day. Interestingly, Gerald Ford became President of the United States the next day when President Nixon resigned in disgrace over the Watergate Scandal. Vice President Ford presented me with a pair of official Vice-Presidential cufflinks. (Maybe he figured that he wasn't going to be needing them much longer.)

Following the brunch, everyone gathered on the front steps of the Hall of Fame building for the speeches. The inductees gave their talks in alphabetical order: Canadeo, George, Groza, and Lane was the order in 1974.

When Paul Brown finished introducing me with his gracious remarks, I immediately received a standing ovation. The response moved me to tears, and I choked up more than several times during my acceptance speech. When it's your turn to speak you're overwhelmed with the emotion of the occasion. It is extremely difficult to say what you really want to say. And there are so many people to thank—teammates, coaches, and teachers—that you don't want to leave anyone out.

I was particularly glad that my mother, despite her poor health, was there. Seeing Jackie's mother, Esther Robbins, and my wife's brother, Rollie, and his wife, Sandy, felt great. But nothing topped the excitement of having Jackie and our children in attendance.

Dante Lavelli and many of my former teammates, rivals, and coaches joined in the celebration. Art Modell also appeared to congratulate me.

Today they put a time limit on the speeches. They've also moved up the parade time to 7:00 AM so as to not interfere with the annual (televised) exhibition game at Fawcett Stadium. Now, after the parade the presenters and inductees go directly to the platform for the speeches and then to the brunch.

I think that today's inductees don't fall apart as much at the podium because before they speak they are teased by their peers about the possibility of crying at the microphone. And, subsequently, they try to control their emotions so as to show those peers that they can get through the talk without breaking up. They see this as a kind of challenge. But every year at least one inductee has trouble completing his presentation without pausing to wipe some tears away or stopping to cry uncontrollably. I can empathize with these guys.

Jackie and I attend the Hall-of-Fame induction ceremonies each year. I see a lot of the old guys I played with, and I am reunited with many dear friends.

The Hall of Fame weekend was a rush of activity. You're kept busy as you move from one event to the next. (In addition to the official Hall-of-Fame schedule of events, for instance, we squeezed in a dinner given on my behalf at the hotel by Ashland University.) You stay up late and rise early—you follow a tight time schedule.

I didn't realize the full scope and magnitude of being a member of the Hall of Fame until I got home to Berea, where our neighbors hosted a dinner for us. Then what I had accomplished finally hit me.

The Hall-of-Fame ceremonies made me appreciate how blessed I had been to have the chance to play football for a great coach, Paul Brown, and a great organization, the Cleveland Browns. I also understood how my teammates (in high school, in college, and in professional football) had challenged and supported me over the years to play the best football that I could play. I finally realized that my success as a professional football player really started with the my parents and brothers. Without their guidance and love no one would have heard of Lou Groza. And, finally, I learned that anything that I did accomplish on the field was a gift from God. He has been the force that has been the most responsible for my achievements on and off the gridiron.

The recognition that I received from countless fans for my football exploits has been quite satisfying and humbling. I collected hundreds of wonderful congratulatory letters from people all over the country, many of whom I didn't even know.

Vince Costello, teammate a close friend, sent us a memory book of clippings and photographs. Sally (his wife) and Vince had made this most treasured gift as a family project.

Enshrinement in the Pro Football Hall of Fame in 1974—the pinnacle of my football career. *Pro Football Hall of Fame*

I know also that I've been fortunate to be in the right place at the right time. I appreciate the role of luck and timing in reaching one's goals in life. I recognize, for instance, that there are many retired players, living and deceased, who are as deserving as me of being enshrined in the Hall of Fame. They may not have received enough votes only because they played on poor teams and therefore were not as visible to the voters. Playing for a tradition-rich and successful franchise like the Cleveland Browns brought me the exposure which led to being recognized.

Being inducted into the Pro Football Hall of Fame is the ultimate honor for any football player. All the effort and sacrifices and hard work was worth it . Again, my induction undoubtedly represented my greatest achievement in football.

Playing football was something that I enjoyed; that's the reason why I did it for so long. The Pro Football Hall of Fame wasn't even an idea when I began playing competitive football, so I was not motivated to excel in my sport by the prospect of enshrinement. But as I got older and reviewed my career (and when the doors to the Hall of Fame opened in 1963) I started to entertain the possibility of one day being in the Hall. And in 1974 I was granted that rare opportunity.

Another treat of residing in the Hall is that I will have left behind a legacy (after I'm gone) of my football accomplishments to my grandchildren and their grandchildren. And when they visit Canton to see my bust and plaque, at the very least, they'll know what I looked like.

* * *

I'm one of very few football players who have been publicly recognized on his home field twice. I have already described "Lou Groza Day" in 1962, but I enjoyed another public tribute when the Browns retired my #76 in a ceremony at Cleveland Stadium on December 1, 1968.

Jackie and our kids stood alongside me as I raised my white #76 jersey to the appreciative thousands at the Stadium. I spoke to the crowd and thanked all of those who made this moment possible. I struggled to hold back the tears. Woody Hayes, the mayor of Martins Ferry, and my mother also were next to me during this emotional farewell. After I talked to the fans, my family and I rode in a car which circled the Stadium. I realized that this would be the last time that I would hear the cheers of a huge hometown crowd.

I harbor very few disappointments or regrets. But losing those consecutive championship games in 1951, 1952, and 1953, was difficult. And losing to Summerall and the Giants in 1958 and to the Packers in the 1965 title contest was tough. But the Browns more often were the victors.

On December 1, 1968, the Cleveland Browns retired my number. Woody Hayes stands behind me.
Norbert J. Yassanye. The Plain Dealer

George Blanda, a straight-ahead kicker like myself and the leading scorer in NFL history, once facetiously mentioned to me: "If America had tightened up on the immigration laws, Lou, we could still be kicking." Jan Stenerud, football's second leading scorer and the greatest of the soccer-style placekickers, eventually helped to make my technique an anachronism.

George Blanda, Jan Stenerud, and me (left to right)—the three leading scorers in football history. *Pro Football Hall of Fame*

The Gogolak boys, Pete and Charlie, are the ones who brought soccer-style kicking to the game. Pete had kicked in the AFL for two years before joining the Giants in 1966. In that same year, his brother Charlie kicked a record nine field goals in a game for the Redskins. They were successful and with that everyone wanted to try that style to get on a pro team. When I kicked, the only way we knew how to kick was the straight-on style. Youngsters began emulating the soccer style. Then the American soccer kickers began to replace the European-born kickers.

All of today's placekickers kick with the soccer style, and they've proved successful. Although I never kicked a ball like a soccer player, I guess that the way that the soccer kicker strikes the football is an advantage over my style. Soccer kickers have more of a kicking surface on the side of their foot. But I don't how they get the power behind the ball. Their style still seems awkward to me.

My sons all kicked straight-on in high school and college probably because they didn't play soccer. The explosion of youth soccer in this country would not happen until my kids were older. My grandchildren kick soccer style. My style is kind of like the Model T Ford—it was great in its day.

When I was playing I never was concerned with establishing personal records because I knew that my records would eventually be broken. The success that the Browns had as a team for such a long period of time was my greatest record.

From a personal standpoint, I was the first player to go over a thousand points, and I ended up having 1608 points, third best in pro football history. (For a long time I held the record for most points. But all records are meant to be broken.) The single biggest win had to be that dramatic victory over the Rams in 1950 when I kicked that last-second field goal to give us our first NFL championship. My winning free throws in the state high school semi-final game has always meant a lot to me. And being named the NFL's Most Valuable Player in 1954 by *The Sporting News* was a great honor. Yet the high point came in 1974 when I became a member of the Pro Football Hall of Fame.

In my life's journey I have had the special opportunity of being introduced to many influential people and celebrities including American Presidents, movie stars, renowned entertainers, and famous athletes.

On the subject of entertainers, comedian Martin Mull is one of the most avid Browns fans in the world. From nearby North Ridgeville, Ohio, Martin told me that he was always pretending to be Lou Groza when he was growing up. He actually has been given the chance to kick field goals during Browns practice sessions and also at the Stadium. As a young boy, Martin mentioned to me, he once entered a coloring contest in which I was the judge.

I have been lucky to have cities outside of the Buckeye State honor me. I have received a "key to the city" from a variety of places including Lackawanna, Atlantic City, and Niagara Falls. St. Louis treated me to a special day while I was still an active player. The fans in St. Louis presented me with a trophy in honor of my long and productive career. They even flew Jackie to St. Louis for the game (and a dinner afterwards) and presented me with a trophy before the game. This unusual and classy gesture represented a rare occasion because the tribute honored someone not on the home team.

Martins Ferry renamed the main street through town (Route 7) as Lou Groza Highway in 1984.

The town that I have called home for most of my life, Berea, has also acknowledged my contributions to the Browns and to the Berea community by honoring me with the Grindstone Award. Jackie and my entire family knew that I was getting this prestigious local prize, but I didn't. And when I was introduced as the recipient of the Grindstone Award, all my kids and grandkids began walking down the aisle. I was stunned. In my thank you I even forgot some of my grandchildren's names.

Berea has also named a local playing field after me, Groza Field. My kids always enjoyed saying, "We're going to Groza Field to play."

A picture that my youngest son Judd drew in kindergarten, however, ranks just as high on the list of favored distinctions as has anything else. His teacher had asked the students to draw something important about Berea.   The school drove the kids around town to see the various sights (Baldwin-Wallace College, the fire station, etc.), as possible subjects for a drawing.   But Judd crayoned a picture of me to complete the assignment. (Many years later Judd surprised me with a video tribute to me for my 65th birthday. He put a great deal of effort and love into the production. I'll always treasure Judd's special birthday gift for me.)

I was in a Wheaties commercial, in a Desenex commercial, and in a Postum advertisement.   I also did an insurance commercial for USF and G.

The college placekicker of the year award, sponsored by the Palm Beach Sports Authority each December, is in my name. I'm particularly proud of this fact. I get a chance to present the trophy to some very talented young kickers.

Lou Groza Highway.

I don't have anything (myths or lies) to set straight except for the stereotype that reads, "Those placekickers are a breed to themselves." This expression is wrong. In the 1940's, 1950's, and through half of the 1960's, those who kicked the ball in professional football were football players, not just kickers. We didn't just kick; we played other positions also. We had no special treatment. We did everything that the other football players did. Today's kicker has difficulty keeping himself occupied at practice because he is so one-dimensional.

I was an offensive tackle and a kicker for most of my career. Here I am looking to block someone for our back Ken Carpenter against the Bears in 1952.
Cleveland State University Archives

* * *

There wasn't anything I didn't like about being a football player. I loved playing football because it was fun. I got used to winning games and championships at an early age, and the teams that I played for continued to win throughout my adulthood. No doubt winning contributed to the great deal of pleasure I got from the game.

My closest and most cherished friendships have resulted from the game of football. Jackie and I have made lifelong friends through

the game. These friendships are not necessarily with football players but with individuals that we have met because of football. And
through my speaking engagements I have become acquainted with
many wonderful people.

Jim Brown and I have remained good friends long after our gridiron
days ended.

I've overcome my shyness and have enjoyed making public appear-
ances. Years ago (when young kickers still used the straight-ahead
style) I would be invited to various coaches's clinics to teach the fundamentals and mechanics of kicking. While a member of the Browns,
I went to Atlantic City for a football clinic in the off-season with
Vince Lombardi. The coach that Joe Paterno replaced at Penn State,
"Rip" Engle, was there as was Sid Gillman.

I became acquainted with a lot of coaches and young kickers at
these clinics. I put on a kicking clinic for kids in Winter Haven, Florida. On occasion I used to go up to Michigan State for Duffy Daugh-
erty and to my alma mater, Ohio State, where I worked with Dick Van
Raaphorst. He later kicked with San Diego. I worked with Jim Mar-

tin who kicked with Detroit and Tom Rogers from Baldwin Wallace College, who had a tryout with Dallas. Rick Rose, now a doctor, was going to Columbia when I helped him. Another Ivy Leaguer, Bryan Clarke of Yale, who acted on *General Hospital* and *Eight Is Enough,* asked for some tips. Jay Spiegel and Dick Abel also visited me in Berea. These guys would call, and then I would take them to the field at Berea High. They were, of course, all straight-ahead kickers. When soccer-style kickers took control of the game, my services as a tutor were no longer needed.

The Browns organization, like all clubs, has made its share of poor decisions, including trading Hall-of-Fame defensive ends Doug Atkins to the Chicago Bears and Willie Davis to the Green Bay Packers. The Packers received two other outstanding defensive linemen from us, Henry Jordan (another Hall of Famer) and Bill Quinlan, who helped to make Green Bay the NFL most dominant team of the 1960's. Trading Hall-of-Fame wide receiver/halfback Bobby Mitchell to the Washington Redskins obviously hurt, but the Browns could not have known that Ernie Davis, the splendid college running back who was drafted by us in exchange for Mitchell, would have died before even taking one hand off. Another poor deal involved sending Paul Warfield to the Miami Dolphins before the 1970 season to draft quarterback Mike Phipps from Purdue. Warfield later returned to the Browns, but his best years were behind him. The players never questioned these decisions. If private discussions were going on among the players about these moves, then I didn't hear about them.

A lot of things go into these decisions that we don't know about. When we got rid of Quinlan, Davis, and Jordan, for instance, we were loaded with quality defensive linemen. We had Len Ford, Paul Wiggin, Bob Gain, and Don Colo.

* * *

Jackie and I started our family when Jeff was born in 1953. Daughter Jill arrived in 1954; Jon in 1955; and in 1961, Judd. All the boys are named Louis. Louis Jeffrey, Louis Jonathon, Louis Judson. We call them all by their middle names. Laurie Jill is our daughter's birth name.

Those were great times—when our kids were young. I have many fond memories. I recall joining Indian Guides with the boys. I'd pretend to be an Indian guide by the name of Big Wind. The kids coined their own names: Jeff was Little Wind; Jon was Cool Breeze, and Judd was Little Breeze.

Going to father/daughter dances with Jill is a fond memory as is all those slumber parties.

One year we drove to California as a family to a Pro-Bowl game, the day after Christmas. The entourage consisted Jackie and me, our three children and a babysitter. The station wagon was packed.

The trip went smoothly until we reached Oklahoma City. Heading west out of Oklahoma City, about 5:00 PM, I was determined to get to one more town before we stopped for the evening. Well, it started sprinkling. Then the sprinkling turned into freezing rain, and soon cars were backed up in an endless line. We learned later that the traffic problem was caused by a jackknifed truck. Late that evening we finally got to the next town, Weatherford.

By the time we got to Weatherford, all the motels were full. I asked this fellow if he had any room in his motel and he said no. One or the workers working on the road saw my plight and said that we could use his room. Jackie, Jill, and the babysitter slept in that room. And I slept with my sons in the lobby. Jackie didn't sleep all night. The boys thought that they were in a jungle; there were cottage cheese boxes filled with plants and hanging vines. We ate breakfast, got in the car and took off. What an experience!

I once gave a speech in Watertown, New York, and took the family along to enjoy some skiing. (We even got snowed in there, and our kids missed some school.) One afternoon Jackie and I watched a young skier who was apparently having more than a little difficulty in trying to control his skis. He was yelling, "Mom! Mom! Mom!" He had dropped his ski poles and was really sailing down the slope.

"Look at that crazy kid! " I shouted.

Then I realized that the young kid was my son—Jon. We thought he was going to go right into the window of the lodge, but he somehow stopped himself just before smashing into the side of the building.

All three of my sons played football at Berea High School. Jeff played tight end, and Jon played defense. They both played football at Ashland University. (My daughter Jill also graduated from Ashland, and three were on campus at one time, for a while.) Ashland fielded very strong teams and Jackie and I enjoyed traveling around the state to watch them play. Jon broke his finger just before he was ready to leave for training camp one year, so, not wanting to get off to slow start, he decided to join the judicial board as he planned to attend law school in the future.

My youngest child, Judd, achieved much success on the gridiron. In high school his Berea team made it all the way to the state championship game. In his senior year Judd won the Lou Groza Award, a prize given to the most valuable football player in the entire Cleveland area. I can't adequately describe the joy I felt when I presented this prestigious award to my own son.

Judd played football at Ohio State but ruptured his disc, which required back surgery. (Retired coach, Woody Hayes, was the first person to visit Judd.) After being red-shirted a year because of the disc surgery, Judd returned only to injure his knee. I remember when Jackie and I went down for homecoming weekend hoping to watch Judd play. At the Friday night pep rally at Ohio Stadium, we had difficulty finding him until we noticed Judd standing down on the sidelines supported by crutches. We stayed over in Columbus while the doctors operated on his knee. Any hopes of Judd playing professional football ended. But his 3.8 point average and fine education insured a successful future in business.

Jackie and I are blessed with eleven grandchildren. The families all live in Ohio. In North Canton, Jeff and Linda Groza have five children—Jessica, Justin, Jenny, Zachary, and Alexis. Jill and Fred Schubert live in Medina with their two sons, Ben and Jeb. Jon and Karen Groza reside in Avon Lake with Jonathon and Abbey. Judd and Laura Groza live in Upper Arlington with Emily and Molly.

* * *

When I played football I was always preparing for "the day inevitable," the day when I would have to retire and find another way of making a buck.

During the war I had been a surgical technician. If I had not been a given a chance to be a football player, then I probably would have gotten into medicine. I probably would have become a doctor. But my college studies led me to another vocation.

After signing with the Browns in 1946 I returned to Ohio State in the off-season to pursue a degree in marketing. I'd go to Ohio State in January and then for six weeks in the summer. I eventually graduated in 1949.

I looked around for a couple of years until someone asked me if I'd be interested in beginning a career in the insurance business. The salary and schedule seemed ideal. I could even work during the regular season because we were off on Mondays and Tuesdays. And I could work full-time at the job during the off-season. (Little did I expect, however, that "the day inevitable" wasn't going to arrive until I completed my twenty-first season.)

Specifically, I am an insurance counselor, an advisor who handles a client's entire insurance program. The contacts that I made through football helped to make for a lucrative career choice. I still go to work everyday. I don't know the word retirement according to my wife.

* * *

The current Browns are working hard at putting a team together that will win the Super Bowl, the ultimate goal of any NFL team. A great football team, like the Browns teams that I played for, needs a certain nucleus of players on the roster who are going to carry the squad from year to year. Today, free agency has affected this winning formula. Unlike my playing days, it's tough to hold on to key players. The salary cap also makes keeping a nucleus of talented players difficult. These factors provide an impressive challenge for any team to remain consistently on top.

* * *

I have enjoyed life. God has blessed me with caring parents, a loving wife, wonderful children, dear grandchildren, and with enough talent and good health to play professional football for over twenty years. I feel grateful and fortunate for all of the gifts that I have received.

Quite early in life I learned that the one of the basic requirements toward success in life is the ability to master the fundamentals of education. I know that this simple philosophy sounds cliche, but good study habits build a base, a foundation, by which a young person can establish and develop goals. As academic, athletic, and personal goals are reached in high school and college, the student acquires the skills necessary to achieve objectives in his or her career after graduation.

For instance, I quickly learned that to become a better high school, college, and professional football player, I needed to spend lots of time practicing the fundamentals of blocking, tackling, and kicking. I was graded on how well I blocked, tackled, and kicked. Anyone who expects to excel at a certain sport or in a certain career must study and apply the fundamentals.

I, therefore, became very fundamental in my approach to life. Because my parents cared deeply for me (and knowing how their concern was responsible for giving me direction and self-confidence) I understood that the greatest gift that I could give to my own wife and family was my love and devotion. I've committed myself to being a good husband, father, and grandfather. And now as I watch my grandchildren grow up I see how my children have assimilated the "fundamentals" of parenting.

We've all heard the expression, "A tall building needs a strong foundation." Likewise, success in life is developed at an early age. Parents who have strong relationships with their kids will raise successful and happy children who later will become successful and happy adults. When a child knows that he or she is loved, that he or she is important enough to discipline, to make sacrifices for, and to give advice to, children, instinctively, fundamentally, will do just about anything to please their parents.

I like to tell young people: "If you work hard, and play hard, then someday you will reap the benefits." This motto has worked for me.

AFTERWORD (Extra Points)

Monday, November 6, 1995 will be remembered as the darkest day in Cleveland sports history, the day it was announced in a Baltimore parking lot (the future sight of a new football stadium) that the Cleveland Browns—**our Browns**—were leaving our city.

The team that I started with in 1946 and played on for 21 years will no longer be the Cleveland Browns. I am shocked and saddened by the news which was thought to be only a rumor.

While I watched the televised press conference, I began to reminisce. I recalled my first game in Cleveland Stadium, the thrill of winning our championship games here, the day the Browns retired my number #76, and the camaraderie among all of my teammates. It is all gone.

Surely we will wake up to find that this has been just a bad dream. We will still be rushing to the stadium in time to watch the players warm-up, to see our Browns and our wonderful fans, and to enjoy a hot dog, a hot chocolate and the halftime show.

The Cleveland fans are the best in the country. They are angered and hurt to see this legacy come to an end.

I love the old stadium with the view of Lake Erie. I'll miss the fireworks displays and the tremendous volume of 80,000 spirited Browns rooters. I'll even miss the stiff winds that often swirled through this cavernous facility. This is our stadium. So much of our lives have been spent here, cheering our beloved team.

I will do my best in any way that I can to help Cleveland land another NFL franchise. We must pull together and acquire an expansion team rather than steal a team from another city. We shouldn't hurt fans from any other city as we have been hurt.

We must provide a team (if not for us) for our grandchildren and their children. We need a team for all the little boys who want to grow up to be Bernie Kosar or Jim Brown.

Say it isn't so.

THE CO-AUTHOR

A lifelong Clevelander, Mark Hodermarsky has edited two books on sports in Cleveland—*The Cleveland Sports Legacy, 1900-1945*, and *The Cleveland Sports Legacy Since 1945*. He teaches English at St. Ignatius High School in Cleveland and offers a course titled *Baseball Literature* .

Groza and Hodermarsky.